THE
MARIAN
PROFILE

Brendan Leahy

THE MARIAN PROFILE

In the Ecclesiology of
Hans Urs von Balthasar

New City Press
New York London Manila

Published in the United States by New City Press
202 Cardinal Rd., Hyde Park, NY 12538
www.newcitypress.com
©2000 Brendan Leahy

Cover design by Nick Cianfarani

Library of Congress Cataloging-in-Publication Data:
Leahy, Breandan, 1960-
    The Marian profile : in the ecclesiology of Hans Urs von Balthasar / Brendan Leahy.
        p. cm.
    Includes bibliographical references and index.
    ISBN 1-56548-139-9 (pbk.)
    1. Mary, Blessed Virgin, Saint--Theology. 2. Balthasar, Hans Urs von,
    1905--Contributions in Mariology. 3. Church. 4. Balthasar, Hans Urs von,
    1905--Contributions in ecclesiology. 5. Catholic Church--Doctrines.   I. Title

BT613 .L43 2000
232.91'092--dc21   99-086076

Bible quotations are from *The Revised Standard Version*
©1966 National Council of the Churches of Christ.

Printed in Canada

Contents

Introduction

"May They All Be One"

In one of his final works, *Our Task,* von Balthasar refers to the greatest wish expressed by Jesus Christ in his prayer to the Father the night before he died, "May they all be one, even as you, Father are in me, and I in you" (Jn 17:21). Jesus' prayer for unity reveals the purpose of his whole life, namely, to gather us into one with God and with one another. His prayer reminds us that this unity is a gift; it is not something we can give ourselves. Moreover, the unity Jesus prays for is not uniformity. It is a unity modeled upon and indeed a sharing in the very life of the tri-une unity of God. Just as in the Trinity there are three divine Persons who are one, the Church Jesus founded as the sign and instrument of unity in the world contains many dimensions or aspects which inter-relate with one another in unity. To bring this reality about, the Church has been gifted with two principles of holiness which shape her life, namely, the Marian and the Petrine principles.[1] This book will examine the Marian principle.

The word "principle" is not directly defined by von Balthasar. He uses other words such as "profile" or "dimension" to convey the same notion. Broadly speaking, when he speaks of principles in the Church, he is referring to fundamental dimensions of the very nature of the Church. Recalling the role of Peter, for instance, he refers to the Church's hierarchical and institutional dimension as the "Petrine principle." The Marian principle, on the other hand, is that dimension of the Church which continues and echoes Mary's yes to God. It

---

1. *Our Task,* 123.

9

is a yes repeated throughout the centuries and the whole people of God, both lay and clergy alike. More specifically, it is evident in the holiness of love and gospel life that continues in the heart of the Church as a unifying force together with the Petrine principle.

The theme of the Marian principle can be found in von Balthasar's earliest writings. For instance, in the years following the worst war the world has ever seen, he wrote a programmatic work entitled *Razing the Bastions* in which he heralded a new era of the Church opening up in the new epoch of world history, an era characterized by a striving toward unity on various levels. Foreshadowing the Second Vatican Council, he pointed to the need for everyone in the Church, lay and ordained, to increase our mutual love and to live outside ourselves. He urged Christians on to be directed toward God and to move beyond narrow confines toward their brothers and sisters in the world. He advocated a rediscovery of the true nature of the Church's catholicity and a true renewal of openness to other Christians, other world religions and people of other convictions. It is in this context that he pointed to Mary.

In returning to the start of the gospel adventure, he meets this woman of the gospel in the little house of Nazareth where the whole Christian movement finds, as it were, its inspiring spark. Throughout his writings, von Balthasar proposes that we look to this woman as a model for all. In saying this, he is not advocating more devotions, feast-days or special prayers. By pointing to Mary he is directing us to where inner vitality gives life to all the traditions of the Church, not in an anachronistic manner, but in what he calls a "breath-taking adventure."[2] Von Balthasar's aim is not merely to have us look at Mary as a personal model of discipleship. The embedding of the chapter on Mary into the Second Vatican Council's constitution on the Church calls for something more. This "milestone" invites a renewed recognition of the Marian principle

---

2. *A Short Primer for Unsettled Laymen* (San Francisco: Ignatius Press, 1985), 17.

operative in the very life of the Church from generation to generation. By highlighting it, von Balthasar wants to encourage an understanding of the Church's identity in terms of a dynamic bi-polar movement within the people of God between the two principles of unity, the Marian and the Petrine.

Von Balthasar's Original Contribution to Ecclesiology

It is not an exaggeration to say that von Balthasar's own life was in no small way dedicated to promoting the "explosive spiritual energy of holiness" associated with the Marian principle. His writings reflect this passion. Although he expressly dedicated only two short works to Marian themes, *The Threefold Garland* (1977) and *Mary for Today* (1987), nevertheless, as Medard Kehl recognizes, the Marian principle in the Church is a nodal point of his thought around which the whole of his theological speculation flows.[3]

Andrew Louth too comments that although explicit Marian dimensions in what can be considered as an overture to von Balthasar's works, *Heart of the World* (1945), are muted and few, this does not alter the fundamentally Marian structure of the work.[4] Far from being a peripheral aspect, the Marian principle is a central viewing-point in his ecclesiology.[5] Not surprisingly, therefore, we discover that already in 1944 von Balthasar published his first article relating specifically to the theme of Mary and the Church,[6] and one of his last works published posthumously in 1988 emphasized Mary's role in the

---

3. Medard Kehl, *Kirche als Institution: Zur theologischen Begründung des institutionellen Charakters der Kirche in der neueren deutschsprachigen katholischen Ekklesiologie* (Frankfurt: Verlag Josef Knecht, 1976), 248.
4. "The Place of *Heart of the World* in the Theology of Hans Urs von Balthasar," in John Riches, *The Analogy of Beauty* (Edinburgh: T&T Clark, 1986), 147-163, espec. 150.
5. Matthias Hembrock, *Die Ekklesiologie Hans Urs von Balthasars: Das Marianische Prinzip in der Kirche* (Münster: unpublished doctoral thesis, 1986), 2.
6. "Die Erscheinung der Mutter," 73-82.

salvific and ecclesial drama.[7] Various writers have been attracted by his writings on the theme.[8] They see his thought as an acquisition for contemporary ecclesiology. In the words of one of these authors, "in the final analysis, it is perhaps the Marian dimension of the Church which is his most personal and original contribution to ecclesiology, and in which his *kairós* to a large degree consists."[9]

The *kairós* in which we find ourselves is marked by transition. In the light of the Second Vatican Council we have moved into the third millennium. Henri de Lubac, an admirer and mentor of von Balthasar's and himself a great theologian, once wrote that the work of this perhaps "most cultivated man" of our time is the most helpful and resourceful in exploiting the treasure of the Second Vatican Council.[10] The highest recognition that this is indeed the case in terms of the Marian principle in the Church comes in Pope John Paul II's encyclical on the dignity of woman, *Mulieris Dignitatem,* published in 1988. The Pope expressly cites von Balthasar in reference to the Marian profile of the Church.[11]

---

7. *Wenn ihr nicht werdet wie dieses Kind* (Ostfildern: Schwabenverlag, 1988).

8. See Wilheim Link, *Gestalt und Gestaltlosigkeit der Kirche: Umrisse einer Personal-Geistlichen Kirchenlehre bei Hans Urs von Balthasar* (Rome: P.U.G., 1970); Joseph Fessio, *The Origin of the Church in Christ's Kenosis: The Ontological Structure of the Church in the Ecclesiology of Hans Urs von Balthasar* (Regensburg University, 1974); Medard Kehl, *Kirche als Institution* 239-311; Achille Romani, *L'Immagine della Chiesa "Sposa del Verbo" nelle Opere di Hans Urs von Balthasar* (Rome: P.U.L., 1979); Johann Roten, *Im Zeichen der Ellipse: Ein Beitrag zur theologischen Anthropologie Hans Urs von Balthasar, unter besonderer Berücksichtigung seines marianischen Denkens* (Dayton, 1987); Michel T'Joen, *Maria, Kerk-in-oorsprong: De Mariavisie van H. U. von Balthasar tegen de achtegrond van de mariologische ontwikkelingen in de twintigste eeuw* (Louvain-la-Neuve, unpublished doctoral thesis, 1986 [for a published extract, see *Marie et l'ésprit dans la théologie de Hans Urs von Balthasar* (Louvain-La-Neuve, 1988)]; Ignace de la Potterie, *Mary in the Mystery of the Covenant* (New York: Alba House, 1992).

9. Fessio, *The Origin of the Church,* 383.

10. "A Witness of Christ in the Church: Hans Urs von Balthasar" *Communio* 2 (1975), 228-249.

11. *Mulieris Dignitatem* (15 August 1988), 27, fn. 55: *AAS* 80 (1988) II, 1653-1729, espec. 1718. The citation from von Balthasar is taken from *New Elucidations,* 196.

Writing about von Balthasar's Writings

Setting out to write a book on von Balthasar's perspectives on the Marian principle in the Church is a daunting task. Anyone who has attempted to communicate something of his thought on any topic knows the difficulty of trying to outline his work without betraying it. Concentrating on only one element, and thus limiting oneself to only a part of the whole vision (which he always attempted to present in each fragment of his writings), seems to run counter to his methodology.[12] That the undertaking is valid is however confirmed by an encouraging word addressed to Kossi K. Joseph Tossou as he undertook a synthesizing work on von Balthasar's pneumatology. Recognizing that his own writings on the theme of pneumatology were like an "archipelago of fragments," von Balthasar wrote that a work drawing it together was worthwhile.[13]

This book then wants to facilitate the reader's journey through another "archipelago of fragments," this time on the theme of the Marian principle in the Church. The approach taken will be thematic because, as commentators such as Vorgrimler, Henrici, Biser, and Wiederkehr have recognized, one cannot really speak of major shifts in von Balthasar's thought during his life. The task at hand is to extract and present both the explicit references as well as the fragmentary intuitions and hints found hidden in the galaxy of his theological work.

---

12. See *Theologik I* (Einsiedeln: Johannesverlag, 1985), VIII.
13. *Streben nach Vollendung: Zur Pneumatologie im Werk Hans Urs von Balthasar* (Freiburg: Herder, 1983), VII.

Adrienne von Speyr

To tell the tale of von Balthasar's life history would be to tell much of his theology, ecclesiology and Mariology. A number of publications in recent years have contributed to our acquaintance with his life-story, so it is not necessary to rehearse it again here.[14] However, one person who played a major role in von Balthasar's life ought to be mentioned: Adrienne von Speyr.

It is well known that von Balthasar's life and theological world is inseparably linked with Adrienne von Speyr. In the introduction to Adrienne's life, work and writings, Barbara Albrecht speaks of the link between them in terms of a double mission of the mystic and her confessor. Von Balthasar was also more than a sacramental confessor. He was the interpreter of her writings whose task it was to make her work fruitful for the Church.[15]

In 1965, von Balthasar himself wrote that Adrienne von Speyr's work and his own cannot be separated; they are two halves of a whole.[16] She was a Protestant medical doctor, widowed and married again in 1936 to Professor Werner Kaegi, the biographer of the famous historian Jacob Burckhardt. Received into the Catholic Church in 1940 by Hans Urs von Balthasar, then a student chaplain in Basel and her spiritual director, it soon emerged that Adrienne had a mission or charism as a mystic in the Church.[17] In Peter Henrici's words,

14. See Medard Kehl and Werner Löser, *The Von Balthasar Reader;* David Schindler (ed.), *Hans Urs von Balthasar: His Life and Work* (San Francisco: Ignatius Press, 1991); John O'Donnell, *Hans Urs von Balthasar* (London: Geoffrey Chapman, 1992); Bede Mc Gregor and Tom Norris (eds.) *The Beauty of Christ* (Edinburgh: T&T Clark, 1994).
15. Barbara Albrecht, *Eine Theologie des Katholischen: Einführung in das Werk Adriennes von Speyr.* Vol. 1: *Durchblick in Texten* (Einsiedeln: Johannes Verlag, 1972); Vol. 2: *Darstellung* (Einsiedeln: Johannes Verlag, 1973), espec. 2:62ff. See also Hans Urs von Balthasar (ed.), *La Missione Ecclesiale di Adrienne von Speyr: Atti del II Colloquio Internazionale del pensiero cristiano* (Milan: Jaca Book, 1986).
16. *Rechenschaft 1965* (Einsiedeln: Johannes Verlag, 1965), 35.
17. See Hans Urs von Balthasar, "Il carisma di Adrienne," in *La Missione Ecclesiale di Adrienne von Speyr,* 179-184.

von Balthasar accepted her insights into scripture and tradition with "theological knowledge and a childlike simplicity of faith."[18] After her death in 1968 he continued to work fervently to promote an appreciation of her mission in the Church.

A glance through his work *Our Task* will suffice to be immediately struck by how prominent the Marian theme is in their common biography. Significantly, Adrienne's first published book was a Marian one, with a chapter on the Marian principle in the Church.[19] Stimulating comparison can be made between Adrienne's *Mary in the Redemption* (1979) and von Balthasar's treatment of Mary in the fourth volume of *Theo-Drama*. Her hidden influence is also to be seen in the areas of patristic studies, the theology of the sexes and Mariology.[20] While all of this is of interest and relevancy, an analysis of the influence of Adrienne's work upon von Balthasar's is beyond the specific task at hand. It must be entrusted to another writer. But that is not to say that we will ignore her influence. References to her works are provided here wherever appropriate.

The Book Before You

In *part 1* the reader is offered an historical perspective, tracing reflection upon the emergence of the Marian principle in the Church throughout the centuries. In *part 2* von Balthasar's own theological framework is outlined with a view to situating his thought on the Marian principle. Of course, Mary is not some abstract principle and so, in *part 3* the salient points regarding Mary and what von Balthasar calls her "theo-dramatic" role will

---

18. Peter Henrici, "Hans Urs von Balthasar: A Sketch of his Life," in David Schindler (ed.), *Hans Urs von Balthasar*, 7-43, here 23.
19. *The Handmaid of the Lord* (London: Harvill Press, 1956), 148-153.
20. *Our Task* 73ff. See also, *First Glance at Adrienne von Speyr*.

be sketched. *Part 4* is a direct consideration of the Marian principle as a constitutive principle of the Church. Finally, *part 5* suggests, on the basis of von Balthasar's writings, some concrete signs of the Marian principle in the Church today.

Part 1

Milestones along the Way

Taking the gospel as his starting point for so much of his reflection on the Church, von Balthasar meditates on the fact that Jesus is not an isolated individual. We see him constantly in relationship with others. He is surrounded on earth by Mary his mother, John the Baptist, Peter and the apostles, the sisters of Bethany and many others. Together these people form what von Balthasar calls a "human constellation" around Jesus.

The history of Jesus and his companions is not just of spiritual consequence, it is also full of theological implications. Von Balthasar writes: "The risen Lord, who wills to be present in his Church all days to the end of time, cannot be isolated from the 'constellation' of his historical life."[1] In other words, these companions of Jesus and their faith experiences are not limited to the Church's origins. Peter's mission, for instance, continues in a certain sense in the popes and bishops of the Church. But it is not just Peter who continues. Von Balthasar invites us to rediscover how, through the Holy Spirit, others too "have founding missions and, in their own way, have no less a continuing life and representation in the Church."[2] In particular, Mary.

So what became of Mary, the mother of Jesus? How has her founding mission continued in the Church? More specifically, what does von Balthasar say about this? In the first part of this work we shall attempt to respond to these questions. We will

---

1. *The Office of Peter and the Structure of the Church*, 162.
2. *Office of Peter*, 158.

indicate some of the milestones in the understanding of the
Marian principle along the past two millennia of Church life
which von Balthasar points to in his writings.[3] These pages are
thus an attempt to trace what led up to today's consciousness
of an emerging Marian profile of the Church.

Of course, there have been Mariological "seasons," including waves and counter-waves of Marian devotion and reflection, but for von Balthasar this is no surprise, since Mary is
known from the gospel both for her "lowliness" and her song
"all generations will call me blessed." Along with John Henry
Newman, he asserts that the doctrine concerning Mary has at
its core remained the same from the beginning, but new insights concerning Mary and the Church have been gained
throughout the centuries of living and meditating the gospel.
The purpose of this chapter is not so much to describe the seasons of Marian devotion as to trace the development of the
awareness of the Marian principle within the life of the
Church.

---

3. This part is based primarily on *Explorations in Theology II: Spouse of the Word, passim;*
Explorations in Theology IV: Spirit and Institution, 169-244; *Theo-Drama III,* 292-318; *Office*
of Peter, 183-225.

The Patristic Era
Mary, Mother of Christ and Model
of the Church

The patristic period is von Balthasar's "alma mater" in terms of his theological reflection. Much of his gallery of thought concerning the Marian dimension of the Church is formed in the school of the Church Fathers.[4] His works often refer to their writings, and therefore we need to dwell a little on some of the significant features of this period.

Firstly, a general comment. Such was the strength of the early Church's vibrant and communional experience of the "two or more gathered in his name" (cf. Mt 18:20) that the patristic world never felt the need to construct an analytic doctrine of the Church: one simply *was* Church. "Though many we are one body" (cf. 1 Cor 12) was the reality experienced and lived out day by day. What writings we do have from that era manifest how the Church was perceived as a realm of light and holiness, paradise restored. As early as Clement's second letter to the Romans (c. 96 A.D.) and the Shepherd of Hermas (c. 140 A.D.) this realm of new life in Christ is expressed in terms of feminine imagery.

Consciousness of the feminine identity of the Church grew through a certain extension and amplification of the Bride motif in scripture (especially Eph 5). Gradually, over time, the ecclesial realm was increasingly depicted as a subject on her own, with a womanly beauty, whose form and adornment, feelings and sentiments, destinies, humiliations, and exaltations could be described. This Bride of Christ, the Church, was loved by people above all as their mother who brought them to

---

4. For an excellent presentation on their thought see Luigi Gambero, *Mary and the Fathers of the Church* (San Francisco: Ignatius Press, 1999).

birth in the new world of Christ, nourished them with bread
from heaven, prepared them for their entry into eternal paradise, in short, as the mother who gave them God. The clerical
aspect of the Church was clearly attested from the beginning.
Von Balthasar comments that it stood in a correct relationship
to the Church's whole communional sphere.[5]

But what about Mary? Clearly, the infancy narratives ex-
pounded in Matthew and Luke, and the episodes of Cana and
the cross as expressed by John, aroused interest in the person
and role of Mary right from the beginning. In the second century, because of the threat of Gnosticism which saw matter as
evil, Irenaeus (c. 130–200 A.D.) strongly emphasized Mary's
real motherhood of Jesus. He also drew a parallel between the
disobedient Eve and the obedient Mary, who gave birth to
Christ, the head of the Church. From the time of Justin
(c. 100–165 A.D.) and Irenaeus, in fact, the concepts
"virgin-mother-Church" and "virgin-mother-Mary" are so
intertwined that, in a sense, they cannot be separated.

While the significance of Mary's yes to God begins to be appreciated from the beginning, the implication of this in terms
of Mary and the Church are poorly developed. In general,
when it came to a consideration of Eve as the helpmate or companion of the first Adam, it is not Mary, but the Church who
was seen as the bride and companion of the new Adam, Jesus
Christ, in generating the members of the Church.[6] In other
words, at this stage, Mary was considered as only indirectly
and in a distant way collaborating with the redemption, which
comes from the Son and is mediated by the Church.

Awareness of Mary's motherhood of the faithful remained
largely implicit. The emphasis was on the Church's motherhood, and at best Mary was referred to as the historical model
or type of what the Church now does — generate Christ in the
world. Ambrose commented that all believers, in fact, can become spiritual "mothers" of Christ through their obedience of

---

5. *Office of Peter*, 183ff.
6. H. Coathalem, *Le Parallelisme entre la Sainte Vierge et l'Eglise dans la tradition latine jusqu'à la
fin du XII siècle* (Rome: Anal. Gregor. 74, 1954).

faith: "Do the will of the Father, and you will be the mother of Christ."[7]

Generally, then, there is a subordination of Mary to the Church during the patristic era. Although called "God's bride" or "the Holy Spirit's bride," and although her unique purity and holiness were praised, Mary was seen essentially as a member, albeit eminent, of the body of Christ. This leads von Balthasar to describe as "anonymous" and discreet Mary's presence in the first centuries of Church theology.[8]

There was a reason for this. In theological reflection Mary remained in the background, as it were, until Christ's divine identity was fully expressed in the Council of Nicea (325 A.D.) and his relationship to the Church as redeemer clarified. Subsequently, the Council of Ephesus (431 A.D.) declared Mary to be the *Theotokos* (bearer of God). It was this Christological declaration which opened up further reflection on Mary as the archetype or model of the Church. Mary gave birth physically to Jesus, but that is not something limited to the past. The Church too continues to "give birth" to the presence of Jesus in each new generation. What begins to be understood more fully is that Mary is more than just a symbolic, anticipatory embodiment of what now takes place in the Church. It is in echoing and, in a certain sense, continuing Mary's yes that the Church gives birth spiritually to "other Christs," the members of Christ's body. The Council of Ephesus is a major milestone in all of this development. It is here, von Balthasar contends, that we are at the origins of the intuition that Mary implicitly contains the properties of the Church.[9]

A notion which may have contributed to greater appreciation of Mary's role in the economy of the Church was that of the "ecclesial soul" (*anima ecclesiastica*). Found particularly in Origen (c. 185–254 A.D.) and also in Ambrose (c. 339–397 A.D.), this notion conveyed the sense that every soul darted with the love of Christ blossoms and extends beyond a private

---

7. *Expositio in Lucam* X, 14, 25 (PL 15:1810).
8. *Office of Peter*, 159.
9. See *Theo-Drama V*, 462–469.

consciousness to a Church consciousness. Von Balthasar signals Methodius (d. c. 311) and Origen as being the first to link Mary and the notion of *anima ecclesiastica*.[10]

A Flash of Intuition: Mary and the Church are Identical

Despite the general tendency to see Mary merely as a member of the Church, von Balthasar directs our attention to "a flash of intuition," which is found primarily in the second-century-writings of Irenaeus of Asia Minor, but also in Hippolytus, Tertullian, Methodius and occasionally in Origen, Ambrose and Augustine.[11] Irenaeus links the image of the Church's motherhood in her virginal fruitfulness (baptism) and the virginal fruitfulness of Mary to such a degree that he almost identifies Mary and the Church.[12]

Von Balthasar echoes Müller when he comments that we are struck by Irenaeus' "flash of intuition" in identifying Mary and the Church, because it is the very first stirrings of a theology of the birth of the Logos from the heart of the Marian Church.[13] Ephraem expressed the tendency toward identification in his hymns, and the culmination came in the fifth century in Cyril of Alexandria's (d. 444 A.D.) "fulminating sermon" at the Council of Ephesus.[14]

In Alois Müller's work we can see how Cyril saw Mary as the living, concrete personification of the Church, the universal Church in concrete form. Accordingly, his Litany of Mary

---

10. *Theo-Drama II*, 309-311; *Theo-Drama V*, 463; *Explorations II: Spouse of the Word*, 166-172. See Origen *Cant. hom.*, 1:10 (in W. A. Baehrens, [ed.], *Origenes Werke VIII. Homilien zu Samuel I, zum Hohelied und zu den Propheten, Kommentar zum Hohelied in Rufus und Hieronymus* [Leipzig: Hinrichs, 1925], 8, 41, 13).
11. Hippolytus, *De antichr.* 44-45; Tertullian, *De carne Christi* 17:9ff; Origen, *Joh. comm.* 1, 4, 23 and Methodius, *De sanguisuga* 8:2-3. See *Theo-Drama III*, 303.
12. *Adversus Haereses* IV, 33, 4 and IV, 33, 11.
13. *Office of Peter*, 198-199; *Theo-Drama V*, 462ff. See Alois Müller, "Ecclesia-Mater: Die Einheit Marias und der Kirche," in: *Paradosis* 5 (Freiburg: Paulus Verlag, 1951), 67ff, and Hugo Rahner, "Die Lehre der Kirchenväter von der Geburt Christi aus dem Herzen der Kirche und der Gläubigen" in his work, *Symbole der Kirche, die Ekklesiologie der Väter* (Salzburg: Otto Müller, 1964), 11-87, espec. 60.
14. See *Office of Peter*, 200.

contained acclamations to her which are alternatively personal and ecclesiological: "Let us praise the ever-virgin Mary, that is, the holy Church, and her Son and immaculate Bridegroom."[15] For von Balthasar this is an acknowledgment in principle of what centuries later the German theologian Scheeben will call a *perichòresis* (mutual indwelling) between Mary and the Church, which is so close that one can be fully understood only in and with the other.[16]

Augustine and the "Dove"

Augustine (354–430 A.D.) is one of the great Church personalities admired by von Balthasar. He presents this African Father's thought in an ecclesial-centered perspective.[17] He esteems in particular Augustine's trinitarian horizon. But to von Balthasar's chagrin, Augustine represents what he sees as a minimalist approach to the Mary-Church identification. While one passage in Augustine reads: "Mary . . . is the Mother of his [Christ's] members [which we are] because in love she co-operated with him so that believers should be born in the Church,"[18] his are also the words: "Mary is holy, Mary is blessed, but the Church is more excellent (*melior*)."[19] Although he concerned himself with the parallel between the symbol (physical birth from Mary) and the reality (spiritual birth from the Church) he did not go as far as Irenaeus. He limited himself to the parallel rather than identification:

> Why is Mary the Mother of Christ? Is it not because she has given birth to Christ's members? You to whom I am speaking are Christ's members: Who gave birth to you? I can hear your heart replying: Mother Church.

15. PG 77:996BC. See A. Müller, *Ecclesia-Maria* (Freiburg, 1951), 154.
16. *Dogmatik III* (Freiburg: Herder, 1865), n. 1819, p. 618.
17. See Werner Löser, *Im Geist des Origenes: Hans Urs von Balthasar als Interpret der Theologie der Kirchenväter* (Frankfurt: Knecht, 1976), 136.
18. *De Virginitate* 6 (PL 40, 399).
19. *Sermo Denis* 25.

This holy, venerable Mother is *like* (*similis*) Mary: she
too gives birth and is a virgin.[20]

While regretting that Augustine did not allow Mariology to
influence his ecclesiology more directly, von Balthasar himself, from the perspective of later centuries, attempts to forge a
link between Augustine's vision of the Church and the Marian
principle. He does so by referring to the imagery of love employed by Augustine in describing the Church.

Central to Augustine's ecclesiology was the notion of the
whole Christ *(totus Christus)*, referring to the Church as both
the "Head and Body," the "Bridegroom and Bride."[21] In
Augustine's view, Christ the head works together with the
Church as the bride, who is inseparably linked to him. Echoing
the imagery of lovers found in the Book of Song of Songs (5:2),
Augustine refers to the Church as Christ's "one and only dove"
(columba mea, immaculata mea). On the basis of this little-
considered theme, he developed a dynamic vision of the
Church. In doing so, his writing resonates with the use of the
nuptial category which prevails throughout the Fathers' imagery of the Church, especially the Eastern Fathers such as
Origen and Gregory of Nyssa (c. 330–c. 395), though it is no-
ticeably absent in Maximus the Confessor's thought.[22]

On the one hand, the dove is the whole Church understood
as the "*communio* and community of the saints."[23] Office in the
Church is embedded within this dove. On the other hand, and
more specifically, the dove is that part of the Church where
true mutual love is lived:

> He [Augustine] not only calls that part of the Church
> Columba that is objectively *immaculata*, but he also
> grants the term to the subjectively perfect community
> of love. Of course, he seees the Church as this commu-

---

20. *Sermo Denis* 35.
21. *Das Antlitz der Kirche* (Einsiedeln: Benziger, 1942), 103-139.
22. See von Balthasar's work on Maximus, *Kosmische Liturgie: Das Weltbild Maximus des
Bekenners* (Einsiedeln: Johannes Verlag, 1961), espec. 202.
23. See Yves Congar, "Introduction générale à Saint Augustin: Traités antidonatistes 1," in:
Oeuvres de S. Augustin 28 (Paris, n.p., 1963), 100-109.

nity insofar as she, as the "Bride" and "Body" of
Christ, help to fulfill his work of loving surrender to
save the world by being perfectly united to him.[24]

The dove is formed in the fire of love by the Holy Spirit,
who dwells in the saints. She is a dynamic, fruitful and purify-
ing communion of saints, a force of love, which draws us toward the essential center of the Church where we, in turn, do
our part in sustaining others.[25]

It is in this sense that the Church is the virginal mother of
believers.[26] The dove brings children to the baptismal font and
helps them enter into communion with Christ.[27] Joining people together in love, the Holy Spirit endows the Church, the
dove, with a sanctity of love. And it is in this personal sanctity
to be found at the heart of the Church that the dove is the authentic subject of the full power to forgive sins.[28] When a sin-
ner is reconciled with the Church through the bishop (i.e.,
through penance) it is the dove (*columba*) who pardons along
with the bishop and allows the person to return to the unity of
love. Von Balthasar presents with enthusiasm this dynamic
Augustinian vision of the interior dimension of the Church.[29]

He also seeks, however, to discover where Augustine locates
this ideal-real Church. In the *Civitas Dei*, an outline of which
can be found in his *Confessions*, Augustine speaks of a
super-temporal, original ideal Church. Though not co-eternal,
she adheres to God in chaste love. She is the created wisdom
(Sir 1:4), our home where there is no movement of the ebb and
flow of time (*domus tua, quae peregrinata non est*), our most beloved mother who is above and free (Gal 4:26).[30]

Ultimately Augustine sees the true Church of love existing
only in the end time, the eschatological era of fulfillment in

---

24. *Explorations IV: Spirit and Institution*, 192.
25. *Explorations IV: Spirit and Institution*, 193ff. See also Methodius of Olympia in *Conviv. decem virg., Sermo tertius*, 8.
26. *De div. quaest.* 83: q. 59, 4. See *Office of Peter*, 190.
27. *Ep.* 98, 5.
28. *De baptismate* 6, 4, 6 (PL 43:200).
29. See also *Sermo* 181, 1-7 (PL 38:979-983).
30. *Confess.* XII, 13, 19 and 23.

Christer.[31] It is at this point that von Balthasar becomes disappointed. He would have preferred Augustine to have linked the notion of dove (*columba immaculata*) with Mary and the Marian core of the Church. He regrets that the *columba immaculata,* which in general Augustine did certainly not mean to limit to the heavenly Jerusalem but to be seen as a real part of the Church on earth, was not linked more with his Mariology. In part, this was due to a certain neo-platonic influence, which posited the hypothesis of a Church of pure love at the level of transcendent idea. In part, it was also due to Augustine's focus on Christ the head who contains all, and so distinction from Christ was difficult to maintain.

Nevertheless, what we have in Augustine is the beginning of an understanding of a mystical reality of the Church, which will emerge more explicitly in the Medieval period and be developed by von Balthasar himself. Gradually, it will be realized that the dynamic *communio* at the heart of the Church is also linked to Mary. Thanks to the interior force of the unity of love at the heart of the Church (the Marian center), whoever reaches this interiority also begins to live the law of the unity of love, and so becomes fruitful.[32]

One final word on Augustine. What von Balthasar admires is not only his dynamic vision of the interior heart of the Church but also the fact that Augustine does not end up with the Gnostics, Montanists and Donatists, who assume two churches: one external and fallible, the other pure and true. Neither does Augustine, unlike Tertullian, ever deny the place of the office and sacraments of the Church. Rather, the main focus of Augustine's ecclesiology was on Christ the head, who makes the bride beautiful by emptying himself for her, similar to the ugly root from which the beautiful tree of the Church rises.[33]

---

31. See *Civitas Dei* 18, 48 (PL 41:610-611); *De continentia* 25 (PL 40:361-362); *Sermo* 181:7 (PL 38:983).
32. *De baptismate* 6, 34, 66.
33. See *Enarr in Ps,* 44.3 (PL 36:494-495).

The Church's office and sacraments serve as mediating forms of Christ the head building up this tree.[34] While always insisting on the sacramental side, Augustine emphasized the personal side of the community of love in the mediation of divine grace in the Church. The power to "bind and loose" given to the Church was not a merely administrative or sacramental function (Mt 16:19). Augustine saw the binding and loosing of what today we might call the institutional-sacramental dimension as rooted in the personal holiness of the whole Church.

Subsequently, Denis the Areopagite's notion of the "ecclesiastical hierarchy" also incorporates the official hierarchy into this comprehensive scheme. There is an inner hierarchy of holiness to which the official hierarchy is joined. This is a key element from this period which von Balthasar wants to highlight.

---

34. See *Sermo* 44, 1ff; 62, 8; 95, 4; 138, 6ff; 285, 6 (PL 38:258ff; 412; 582; 766; 1296).

The Medieval Era
Mary, Mother of Believers, Spouse of Our Lord Jesus Christ

Moving on to the Medieval period, a characteristic that can be noted from the Carolingian era onward is a certain discomfort in celebrating the nuptial image of the Church. Given the rather lacerated situation of the earthly Church was it credible to say that the Church is Christ's bride washed clean through the Word? Even the alleged "hypostasis" of a pure Church had begun to lose its previously unchallenged credibility. Von Balthasar contends that this Medieval resignation to an understanding of the Church as not being spotless is the first step toward the "sociological" Church of the present day.[35] People lose sight of the inner radiance of the Church.

There was, however, another development which moved in the opposite direction. It was during this period that attention turned more and more toward Mary. True, prayers had already been addressed to her and churches were consecrated in her honor especially from the Council of Ephesus onward. But in the Medieval era the liturgical Marian feasts and prayers intensified. After all, it was not the Church to which the title *Theotokos* had been given, nor had anyone ever suggested that the Church could be prayed to. So consideration of the historical person of Mary increased, and gradually people saw her as what von Balthasar calls the *Realsymbol* of the pure Church.

This development came about from centuries of living and meditating the gospel. In particular, Mary's yes to God was a source of generations of wonder. A passage from Ambrosius Autpert (abbot of a monastery in Benevento, d. 784 A.D.) writing in the early Medieval period expresses this meditative

---

35. *Office of Peter*, 195.

contact with the annunciation: "O Blessed Mary, the entire entrapped world implores you to say yes; the world makes you, O Mistress, the pledge of its faith. Do not hesitate, Virgin, but hasten to answer the messenger and conceive the Son; have confidence and feel the strength that comes to you from above."[36]

In the twelfth century, Mary's "co-operation" with Christ came into greater prominence. A new milestone was reached at this point. The nuptial category, previously employed in reference to Christ's relationship with the Church now became directed toward the Christ-Mary relationship.

The Church's biblical attributes, especially that of being viewed as "Christ's Spouse" and "New Eve," "helpmate" (companion) of the "New Adam," were transferred to Mary. The Marian-bridal image, especially in the writings of Bernard (1090–1153),[37] came to pervade the commentaries on the Canticle of Canticles. Previously, a mere smattering of verses were applied to Mary, but now the whole text was read with her in mind.

It was at this time that the Church as bride, difficult to grasp in herself as a person, appears, as it were, polarized in the person of Mary, and Mary herself is understood to crystallize around herself the whole community of the faithful.[38] At this point, Mary is no longer viewed as subordinate to the Church. As archetype and real symbol, she is more and more seen as preceding the Church, gathering the Church around her, and standing vis-à-vis (*gegenüber*) Christ.

This period is characterized by von Balthasar as "Christo-typical" in the sense that Mary is seen as Christ's "counterpart." Within this perspective, she is linked more with Christ vis-à-vis the Church than in the "ecclesio-typical" perspective where she is linked more with the Church vis-à-vis Christ.[39] Admittedly, this was never exclusively so, because

---

36. PL 39:2105-2106.
37. See *Glory of the Lord II: Clerical Styles* (San Francisco: Ignatius Press, 1984), 262.
38. See H. Riedlinger, "Die Makellosigkeit in den lateinischen Hoheliedkommentaren des Mittelalters," *BGPhThMA* 38 (1958) n. 3, 71ff; 97ff; 112ff.
39. See *Theo-Drama III*, 305.

the Middle Ages' mystical realism ensured that Mary's ecclesio-typical nature was not forgotten. Mary was never seen merely as an individual in relationship to Christ. There was an awareness that in her unique relationship with Christ, it is the Church as bride which is realized symbolically in Mary.

Mary's Maternal Activity

The Medieval period also emphasized Mary's maternal activity in the Church. We have already mentioned that throughout the patristic era Mary was only implicitly acknowledged as mother of the Church. It is true that Peter Chrysologus described her as "mother of all the living through Christ."[40] But it took several centuries for a deeper realization of what this meant.

In the twelfth century, in the writings of Richard of St. Victor (d. 1173), it became more common to view the Woman of the Apocalypse (Rv 12) not predominantly as the Church but as Mary.[41] More and more it became clear that Mary's immediate and personal relationship with all members of the Church exists not only because of her intercessory power but rather, more specifically, because of the very special character of her yes and co-operation with Christ in generating us as sons and daughters in Christ.

Her eminent educative maternity over all, therefore, began to be celebrated in the Medieval period. An instance of this can be found in Philip of Harvengt (d. 1183 A.D.), a Belgian monk whose writings reflect an Augustinian hue. He never tires of extolling the maternal activity of Mary in the first ages of the Church; Mary bringing forth the apostles as if bearing them and, as the mother of all, presiding over them and, through her constancy in faith, calling the vacillating disciples to order.[42] The German mystics will speak of Mary spreading

---

40. *Sermo* 99 (PL 52:478).
41. PL 196:517.
42. See *Explorations II: Spouse of the Word*, 177.

her protective cloak over the whole of Christendom and making some part of her stainlessness flow out over the bride, the Church.

Regarding these developments, von Balthasar comments that Mary came into prominence at the right time, preventing the disintegration of the idea of the Church into mediocrity and ultimately into sociology.[43] The Church does have a pure center of love. It is Mary and all who live the holiness of love:

> But the person of Mary took over the theological place formerly occupied by the (unreflectedly) "hypostatized" pure Church. In the commentaries on Revelation 12 (Ambrosius Autpert) and on the Song of Songs (Paschasius Radbert), Mary becomes more and more recognized as the one who has been given the "fullness of grace" — *gratia plena* — an archetype of that fullness of grace which Christ has given to the Church (Abélard, Alan of Lille, Albert the Great). The role of Mary at the foot of the cross, where, according to ancient teaching, the Church was born from the wound in Jesus' side, was brought into sharper focus (e.g., by Rupert of Deutz), emphasizing her motherhood with regard to the Church. With her own conception and birth, the seed of the Church has already been planned "because the first person in the Church was born."[44]

So far all is well, because, from Irenaeus via Augustine to Anselm and Bernard, the Marian principle is embraced within the whole realm of Christian dogmatics without any one-sidedness. The problem, however, is in keeping the balance right. The increased attention to the person of Mary during this period is judged as legitimate by von Balthasar in that by giving honor to Mary's role, honor was given to God. Distortions arose, however, when the finite-infinite,

---

43. *Office of Peter*, 202.
44. *Office of Peter*, 201.

creature-Creator distance was forgotten and Mary's place was exaggerated in a wrong manner.

Due to a gradual increase in the attribution of almost Christological and divine attributes to Mary she became isolated as an object of devotion. The exaggerations and distortions regarding her identity which crept in created "a stumbling block, understandably, for Protestants" and "were clearly getting farther and farther away from authentic Catholic tradition."[45] Von Balthasar sees these exaggerations and distortions as a misunderstanding of the Marian principle.

---

45. *Theo-Drama III*, 315.

From the Second Vatican Council Onward
The Marian Principle in the Church

In this chapter we want to examine the period bringing us up to the Second Vatican Council and after. Remote preparation for this must be the shift that took place at the Reformation and other contemporary movements. The most significant feature resulting from the Reformation, the Counter-Reformation, the rise of natural sciences and the Enlightenment was a shedding of attention to the mystical traits of the Church. Focus in ecclesiology gradually shifted to questions concerning the structure and organization of the divided visible Church. The three hierarchical offices became the central form of the Church's manifestation, along with sacraments, liturgy, juridical discipline, and dogmatics as the doctrine of defined dogmas to be believed.

The mystical notion of the Church as a feminine sphere, the "bride of Christ," began to wane. Private devotion to Mary continued. While wrong in its limits, von Balthasar believes this devotion was not wrong in its essence as, deep down, it was a devotion to Mary seen as the real symbol of the immaculate Church. But certainly, this was not clearly manifest.

A new milestone was reached, however, in the Second Vatican Council with the insertion of the chapter on Mary into the Constitution on the Church.[46] Von Balthasar himself summarizes the significance of this shift as follows:

> What in patristic times was (a) largely impicit, that is, Mary's motherhood not only of Christ but also of the faithful — which means that she has a bridal relationship with Christ — becomes (b) explicit in medieval times. However, this extrapolation of Mary leads to

---

46. *Theo-Drama III*, 316-317; *Explorations III: Creator Spirit*, 238-239.

such imbalances that (c) in the Second Vatican Council, while the essential insights gained down through the centuries are held fast, the whole mystery is brought back under the heading of ecclesiology.[47]

Von Balthasar describes the immediate background to this milestone development in terms of a two-pronged dynamism, which preceded it over the 150 years leading up to the Council. It is a dynamism evident in dogmas and apparitions, theological literature and devotion.[48]

Firstly, the role of Peter was more clearly defined. His role had come increasingly into focus due to historical circumstances in the preceding centuries, such as the challenges of Conciliarism, Protestanism, Gallicanism, Jansenism, and Josephism. A need arose for reflection on the Church's charism of indefectibility. This reached what von Balthasar considers a provisional conclusion in Vatican I with the definition of Papal Infallibility.[49]

Secondly, the role of Mary too came into focus in new ways during the nineteenth and the twentieth centuries. Von Balthasar refers us, for example, to Marian apparitions and definitions. In utter humility and in pointing to God's almighty grace, Mary manifested herself in the apparitions as the prototypical Church upon whom we should be modeled.[50] The two Marian definitions, the Immaculate Conception (1854) and the Bodily Assumption (1950) expressed the centrality of Mary's role in the whole plan of salvation.

In an interesting observation, von Balthasar points out that the two Marian definitions form the frame "not by chance" for the Petrine dogma of Infallibility. [51] He sees in this fact an

---

47. *Theo-Drama III*, 300.
48. See also Hanspeter Heinz, "Maria als Ort der Begegnung von Gott und Mensch," *Wissenschaft und Weisheit* 49 (1986), 134-159.
49. See *Office of Peter*, 212-222.
50. *Mary for Today* (Middlegreen: St. Paul Publications, 1987), 43ff; *Homo Creatus Est: Skizzen zur Theologie V* (Einsiedeln: Johannes Verlag, 1986), 160ff; "A proposito di apparizioni" in *La Realtà e la Gloria: Articoli e Interviste* 1978-1988 (Milan: EDIT, 1988), 45-48.
51. *Explorations II: Spouse of the Word*, 23-24.

expression of the all-embracing motherhood of the Marian Church containing the Petrine principle. Reviewing the history of Vatican I and its proposed documents, he believes this Council referred to both a "Marian unity" and a "Petrine unity" in the Church. It was because of war and the consequent interruption of the Council that the "Marian unity" was treated only briefly in the prologue to *Pastor Aeternus*.[52]

The period which followed the First Vatican Council saw a large number of Marian encyclicals and theological literature about Mary. But the "flood of Marian speculation" was too isolated from other theologies to bear fruit that would last. Serious exegetical reflection on the Bible, however, as well as a renewed study of the patristic literature of the relationship between Mary and the Church prepared the turning point which the Second Vatican Council brought about.

The great achievement of this Council, in von Balthasar's opinion, was that in an era of unified planning of the world, the true catholic nature of the Church was liberated from narrow confines. This came about by highlighting the *communion* of life, which lies at the heart of Church identity, and re-locating the Petrine principle within this communion rather than leaving it isolated outside it.

Thus, Vatican I found its completion because, in its decision to place the chapter on Mary into its constitution on the Church, Vatican II highlighted the Marian principle as a vibrant principle within the Church's mission. Mary is not merely a devotion but intimately linked with the formation of the Church-community modeled on the life of the Trinity:

> In summarizing the principal themes of the *Maria-Ecclesia* tradition, the Council points out the differences in Mary's relationship to the three Persons of the Trinity (*Lumen Gentium*, 52-53: "Mother of the Son, therefore . . . daughter of the Father and temple of the Holy Spirit," 65). . . . Most of all, however, Mary's

---

52. Denzinger-Schönmetzer, *Enchiridion Symbolorum* (Rome: Herder, 1976), n. 3051. See *Office of Peter*, 212-222.

work as a "helpmate" of the New Adam is focused wholly beyond herself and subordinated to his trinitarian work of salvation: to make people, i.e., his brothers and sisters, be children of the Father by the gift of the Holy Spirit and thus gather them into a community founded on trinitarian life.[53]

In an article written in the context of the 1985 Extraordinary Synod celebrating, verifying and promoting Vatican II on its twentieth anniversary, von Balthasar is even more explicit about this. Vatican II, he says, highlighted the Church's role as the sacrament of unity with God and of unity among all humankind. This sacrament of unity contains both the exterior Petrine unity and the interior Marian unity. The Petrine unity is the hierarchical principle in the Church. The Marian element of the Church is Mary's spousal-maternal presence providing a Marian unity at the core of the earthly-heavenly Church where the order of nature is fulfilled in grace, *erôs* in *agápe*, the created cosmos in ecclesial love.[54]

After Vatican Council II

Most of von Balthasar's writings on Mary and the Church in the Second Vatican Council present the broad canvas. For the details, he refers us to other scholars.[55] While praising, as we have just seen, the decision to place the chapter on Mary into the document on the Church, and in particular rejoicing in the prominence of the maternal motif, von Balthasar regrets that more attention wasn't paid to the bridal imagery of the Christ-Mary relationship. By failing to give due emphasis to this, von Balthasar senses a risk of "minimalism" in relation to

---

53. *Office of Peter*, 204.
54. "Il Sinodo sul Concilio," *Il Sabato* (Dec. 12, 1985) and reprinted in *La Realtà e la Gloria*, 69-77.
55. See *Theo-Drama III*, 316-318; *Office of Peter*, 202-204. See also Giuseppe M. Besutti, "Note di cronaca sul Concilio Vaticano II e lo schema 'De Beata Maria Virgine,'" *Marianum* 26 (1964), 1-42.

the theme of Mary and the Church. The impression could be that Mary's relationship to believers and their relationship to her consists, prevalently if not exclusively, in a moral sense of contemplation on her sanctity and imitation of her virtues. More attention might have been given to the Christ-Mary relationship in terms of the Marian principle as an operational principle (in and with Christ) in the life of the Church.

Subsequent to the Council, von Balthasar himself worked on a theodramatic Mariology, which would significantly develop this theme. He was mindful of Paul VI's guidelines in *Marialis Cultis* for a true renewal of Marian devotion, which would give due importance to its biblical sources as well as its trinitarian, Christological, ecclesiological and anthropological dimensions.[56] Paul VI's declaration of Mary as Mother of the Church (*Mater ecclesiae*) was echoed in von Balthasar's work on the papacy, *The Office of Peter,* in an important chapter on the all-embracing motherhood of the Church.[57]

Despite his advanced years and the rush to complete his theological trilogy before he died, von Balthasar still found time to write a commentary on Pope John Paul II's encyclical *Redemptoris Mater.*[58] He considered the encyclical to be a synthesis between chapter 8 of *Lumen Gentium* and the topic of Mary and the Church, so much a personal intuition of John Paul II's. In particular he noted the prominence of the nuptial categories applied to the Christ-Mary relationship found in that writing. In von Balthasar's view, by going a few steps further than the Council in what it says about the relationship between Mary and the Church, and in providing a deeper insight into what the Council said, this encyclical is a new opening for Western ecumenism.

Von Balthasar did not live to see Pope John Paul II refer in *Mulieris Dignitatem* to one of his own works in the context of

---

56. Paul VI, Apostolic Exhortation, *Marialis Cultus* (2 February 1974) AAS 66 (1974), 113-168. See von Balthasar's commentary in *Maria, die Mutter des Herrn* (Bonn, 1979), 48ff.
57. *Office of Peter,* 183-225.
58. See *Mary, God's Yes to Man: Pope John Paul II's Encyclical Letter, Mother of the Redeemer.*

writing about the Marian dimension of the Church. In stating that the Church's Marian profile is "also — even perhaps more so — fundamental and characteristic for the Church as is the apostolic and Petrine profile to which it is profoundly united,"[59] the pope clearly paved the way for further study on that intuition which von Balthasar strove so much to highlight. It has been taken up in the Catechism of the Catholic Church (n. 773).

Conclusion

From what we have seen in this first part of the book, von Balthasar considers Mary like a mirror held up ever more insistently before the eyes of a Church that seeks self-understanding. As the centuries pass, people see that she *explains* the Church. She also helps to *bring about* the Church. At the very beginning of our history, she disappeared into the very heart of the ecclesial community as an anonymous but very real presence. Through the centuries there has been an increased awareness and reflection upon the role of Mary in the salvific and ecclesial economy. Today, at the dawn of the third millennium, there is a new and more explicit awareness of the Marian principle in the Church as the sacrament of unity with God and with one another.

---

59. *Mulieris Dignitatem* (15 August 1988), 27, fn. 55: AAS 80 (1988) II, 1653-1729, espec. 1718. See *New Elucidations*, 196.

Part 2

God's "Trinitarian" Logic

On the occasion of von Balthasar's seventieth birthday, Bishop Klaus Hemmerle of Aachen in Germany, himself a former professor of philosophy of religion in Freiburg, wrote him a letter to mark the occasion. It pleased von Balthasar and so Hemmerle subsequently published it as a short book. The introduction offers a brief presentation of von Balthasar's theological method.[1] It is a good starting point for this chapter, which aims to introduce salient features of the theological horizon against which he sketches his writings on the Marian principle in the Church.

Hemmerle comments that von Balthasar's work is an alternative to a merely anthropological presentation of theology. In other words, he doesn't try to fit God, as it were, into human needs and human intellectual possibilities. He doesn't start with a static, self-sufficient metaphysics and then try to work the events of salvation into it. That would be to degrade the marvelous wonders of God who, while adopting our human language and history, is always his own exegete.

There is nothing static or dry about God's revelation; likewise in von Balthasar's writings on the subject. While striking out nothing of what belongs to the fullness of dogma or its conceptual unfolding within tradition, he manages to convey the beauty of its symphonic unity. In his view, tradition is deformed through dissecting it piece by piece in sterile fashion. He is very reluctant, therefore, to create a hermeneutical

---

1. Hemmerle, *Thesen zu einer Trinitarischen Ontologie* (Einsiedeln: Johannes Verlag, 1976), 7-8.

artifice that fragments revelation. His great trilogy — *The Glory of the Lord* (on theological aesthetics) *Theo-Drama* (on theological dramatic theory) and *Theo-Logic* (on theological expression) — is an attempt to present the beautiful, engaging and expressive harmony of the "whole" of divine revelation.

Perhaps this comes as no surprise when we consider his love of the arts. He admired the harmony found in Mozart's music and in the paintings of artists such as Poussin or Grünewald. He was inspired by the cosmic catholicity and love of the "whole" found in the works such as those of an acquaintance like Paul Claudel. The God-nature religion of awe and form found in Goethe appealed to him.[2]

The reader cannot but admire his scholarship. He is careful not to harm the historical and factual elements which scripture vividly puts before us. His appreciation of the speculative skill and precision of decision achieved in patristic and scholastic texts ensure that in his writings they are never banned to the museum. But he is also fully aware of the contemporary changes in the way we understand being and, more specifically, the historical nature of our thinking. He is not one to exclude new developments and leave them outside the door of the Church.

What impacts most upon the reader of von Balthasar's writings is the new style of theological thought which they promote. Forged from the writer's own profound linking of theology and spirituality, he invites us to gaze at reality "from above" but always "earthwards," with a view to being involved in the world "from below" but always "heavenwards." In his theology, writes Hemmerle, both philosophy and spirituality become new. Our thought-structures, the way we see things, and our personal behavior are confronted in theology with something new. Reminiscent of Dante's opening words of the *Paradise*, von Balthasar seems to start from a mystical-theological experience:

---

2. See B. Leahy, "Theological Aesthetics," in Bede McGregor and Thomas Norris (eds.), *The Beauty of Christ*, 23-55.

The glory of Him who moves all things soe'er
Impenetrates the universe, and bright
The splendour burns, more here and lesser there.
Within that heav'n which most receives His light
Was I, and saw such things as man nor knows
Nor skills to tell, returning from that height.[3]

Anyone wanting to dip into von Balthasar's writings has to tune into the melody of one who is returning from that height. But the melody should be familiar to all Christians because, as Hemmerle highlights, von Balthasar does not start from some abstract or strange point of departure but simply from the center of our faith, from the event of Christ read from a trinitarian perspective, an event to which all of creation is linked.

The Christ-event is the "height" we all share in through faith, hope and charity. It is the center from which the beauty, drama and logic of Christian faith unfolds in symphonic fashion. Throughout his writings von Balthasar reflects on how Christ is the point in which the divergent rays of all creation converge. The three central motifs which can be heard throughout the symphony of these writings are mystery, communion and mission, themes that articulate von Balthasar's fascination with God's "trinitarian logic" of love made manifest in Christ, the Word made flesh.[4]

Before proceeding, it is important to recall that while we can "appropriate" mystery to the Father, communion to the Son and mission to the Holy Spirit, von Balthasar always underlines that each of these terms — mystery, communion and mission — finds its fullness in the triune life of God. In other words, the permanent horizon is the loving dialogue-event of the "interaction" between the three divine Persons in the unity of the divine essence. Just as no one of the three divine Persons can be considered without reference to the loving exchange with, for and in the other two, likewise, as we shall

---

3. Dante, *The Divine Comedy 3: Paradise,* Canto I (London: Penguin Books, 1986), 53.
4. The expression "trinitarian logic" is taken from von Balthasar, *Theologik II: Wahrheit Gottes* (Einsiedeln: Johannes Verlag, 1985), 31. See Silvano Cola, "Nuovi orrizonti per la teologia e la pastorale" *Gen's* 28 (1998), 68-73.

endeavor to point out, mystery, communion and mission are always inter-connected.

Mystery

A sense of wonder pervades von Balthasar's writings. In particular, wonder at the ineffable mystery of God revealed to us in Jesus Christ. "For he has made known to us in all wisdom and insight the mystery of his will, according to his purpose which he set forth in Christ" (Eph 1:9). The mystery of God which arouses wonder is not God's hiding from us, but rather the revelation of his "plan for the fullness of time," which is nothing less than "to unite all things in Christ, things in heaven and things on earth" (Eph 1:10).

The Novelty of Christian Revelation

At several points in his work, von Balthasar compares and contrasts the various ways of salvation offered in history, emphasizing the sheer novelty of Christian revelation.[5] Before taking a brief look at some of them, it is good to recall that in an article that von Balthasar wrote on the Marian shape of the Church, he describes the fundamental and universal experience of being born into the world, no matter in which religious context, as one of gratitude.[6]

It is the interpersonal experience which begins for every child when, through the mother's smile, we awaken to a self-consciousness of being accepted and loved. From the love of this human "thou" (the mother) we come to know ourselves as loved and lovable; as being able to go out of ourselves in love. We also know that the "other" who loves us is not the

---

5. *Man in History*, 3ff; *Explorations III: Creator Spirit*, 15ff; *Explorations IV: Spirit and Institution*, 29ff; *Theo-Drama IV: The Action*, 71-201.
6. "Die marianische Prägung der Kirche" in Wolfgang Beinart (ed.), *Maria heute ehren: eine theologisch-pastorale Handreichung* (Freiburg: Herder, 1977), 263-279.

only "other" in the world. Our horizon expands. Gradually we come to learn that our parents are not absolute, that there is some Absolute "thou" to whom I am directed in a mysterious manner.

In fact, together with Plotinus, Augustine, Thomas Aquinas, and Michelangelo, von Balthasar claims the ultimate human disposition is one of nostalgia.[7] We long for a paradise we sense we are made for but which the world seems to deny to us. This dream of paradise always remains with us despite its denial in the myriad of limitations we encounter as we grow.

The nostalgia for paradise is glimpsed in the histories of the world's civilizations recorded in ancient art symbolizations, monuments and literature. When faced with the enigma which our limitations, suffering and death present to us, people have universally refused to resign themselves and to merely being thrown into the world. They strive for a wholeness which takes the constants of our human condition (body-spirit, man-woman, individual-community) seriously. They know this search is bound up with a divine ground.

Ancient pagan religions fashioned mythic accounts of the origin of the world in which a lively role was ascribed to the gods. Tragic conflict and suffering is the way of salvation offered in the mythic framework. The positive feature of myths is that they don't deny the world and use the language of the world with which we are familiar. They present the gods as vibrant personalities involved in cosmic struggle. But, ultimately, in mythic symbolism the divine and human end up bound together within one all-encompassing cosmos and fate. The distinction between heaven and earth flattens out.

The great world religions and the discovery of philosophy (the pure Greek religion) broke through into something new by presenting a vertical, ascending movement toward the Absolute as the way of salvation. God is transcendent and is not to be confused with this world. This vertical approach is aimed at re-gaining a lost "golden era" by climbing out of this world and

---

7. See *Theo-Drama IV*, 116; *Homo Creatus Est*, 9ff.

out of time (all of which is considered appearance) toward the divinity which is perceived to be wholly other (*aliud*) to this world. The price of this vertical way is very high. It involves exclusion of the world, time, corporality and history, in other words, of the very concrete realm in which we live. What's more, the Absolute in which I am to be fulfilled is impersonal, faceless.

With the *Old Testament* something very new emerges. While weaning us off mythic reductions of God to this world, and progressively highlighting God's transcendence, it tells us that the Absolute and Infinite Mystery is not impersonal but, on the contrary, a living and merciful God, who has begun to establish a relationship with us. Unlike the vertical ascending movement of philosophy and the great world religions, the Old Testament tells us that we do not have to climb out of history to meet God, because he has taken the initiative to encounter us in our history. In the story of Abraham we see a God who calls by name, chooses, accompanies and so gives a new identity to Abraham. Later, through Moses, he makes a covenant with Israel as his personal and collective partner.

In this "I–Thou" covenant between God and humanity, a dialogue of salvation unfolds in which there is a positive yes to creation, corporality, the world and time. The fullness of God's overture to us, however, is not in the present but in the future. He has not yet revealed his face. The Old Testament is a horizontal movement of a promise of fulfillment.

"*Jesus Christ* brings total novelty in bringing himself." This is what Irenaeus, the great second-century theologian and bishop of Lyons wrote, and it expresses a key theme in von Balthasar's writings.[8] The novelty of the Christian way of salvation is the Person of Jesus Christ. He himself is the way, the truth and the life. It is by being "in Christ" that, here and now, we can share in the greatest "event" of all — the divine and ever new event of love between the Father, Son and Holy Spirit.

---

8. *Adversus Haereses*, IV:34:1 (Sources Chrétiennes, 100:846-847).

What Christian revelation manifests is that God is not a distant, isolated figure but rather a mutual-being-for-one-another of three divine Persons. God has created and redeemed us in order to give us a share in this threefold gift of life (cf. 1 Jn 1:1-4). And "One of the Trinity" has brought that life among us.

It is in the life, death and resurrection of Jesus Christ that we perceive this new realm opening up for us; we become involved in it, and we find ourselves moving in the Truth. In him, we discover the "breadth and length, the height and depth" of the love of God. Our doorway to God is not, therefore, surrender to tragic destiny as proposed in myth, nor ascetic negation of our world as in some world religions, but rather involvement in an "event" — crossing over through, with and in Jesus to dwell in the bosom of the Father. He who is love incarnate is our doorway to God. Walking in the crucified and risen Christ, our way of salvation does not exclude our corporality, the world and history but rather transforms them through living out his commandment, "love one another, as I have loved you."

Von Balthasar writes that all of our history finds its "place" in the drama of redemption, the drama of God sending his only Son among us. From all eternity, the relationship between the Father and the Son is infinite in love. God created the world in the Word, and in view of the Word made flesh. Accordingly, the "space" between the Father and Son contains all the possibilities of creation within its embrace. Adopting language of the theater, von Balthasar writes of the drama of human history unfolding within the greatest drama of all — the drama of love between Jesus Christ and the Father in the Holy Spirit, which we read about in the gospel.

Two biblical icons express this — Jesus' cry of the cross, representing the depths of human nostalgia, "My God, my God, why have you forsaken me?" and the Easter declaration, expressing the Father's infinite love that fills every emptiness: "You are my Son, today I have begotten you." It is within this dialogue of love between the Father and the Son that here and now "we live and move and have our being" (Acts 17:28).[9] In the words of Simeon the New Theologian, the Father is the home, the Son is the doorway, and the Spirit is the key.[10] That is why the Christian way of salvation proclaims love alone to be credible, because it is when we love that "we pass from death to life" (1 Jn 3:14), life in God.

Encountering the Mystery

From what we have just considered, we can see why for Christianity the encounter with the Mystery involves conversion, turning around, entering into the realm which is freely offered to us in Jesus Christ. In this regard, a comment from Kierkegaard expresses von Balthasar's view. Coming to know God is not like climbing all by ourselves a staircase of a million steps to reach up to him. The "one thing necessary" is the conversion to love. The ever greater God (*Deus semper maior*) is always beyond our expectations but, in his grace, the moment of conversion turns us round to participate in his very love, which opens up to us in Jesus Christ.

In von Balthasar's writings, Mary is like an explanation of all this. She is the paradigm of our encounter with the mystery of God disclosed in Jesus Christ. In her uniqueness, she encounters God in a way which does not eliminate her history, her corporality, her world but rather fulfills and surpasses her dreams. Her yes to God is one of perfect love. She delivers herself over to God. Totally "expropriated," as von Balthasar says, she plays the unique role in history God has for her, and in this she is totally free. She lives outside herself, not making her own limited plans but rather, from the annunciation onward, journeying in the mystery of God opening up in Jesus Christ, a

9. See *Theo-Drama II*, 284ff.
10. *Catech. XXXIII* cited by P. Coda, *Dio Uno e Trino* (Milan: Edizioni Paoline, 1993), 207-208.

journey of unforeseen horizons for her in relation to humanity.

A detail of von Balthasar's own life throws light on the centrality of these themes in his writings. As he continued his studies in his early twenties, he felt a growing emptiness within him. He became disillusioned with what he saw as a modern Promethean attitude to artistic work which puts the artist before the work. "Hacking" his way through the jungle of modern literature in Vienna, Berlin, Zurich and elsewhere, he became more and more disappointed. He compared himself in this period to Habakkuk lamenting and carrying his empty food basket.[11]

A decisive moment came in the summer of 1927 when he went on a thirty-day retreat for lay students in the Black Forest near Basel. Years later he would still remember the tree beneath which "I was struck as by lightning." "It was simply this: You have nothing to choose, you have been called. You will not serve, you will be taken into service. You have no plans to make, you are just a little stone in a mosaic which has long been ready. All I needed to do was 'leave everything and follow' without making plans, without wishes or insights. All I needed to do was to stand there and wait and see what I would be needed for."[12]

For von Balthasar this experience was something of a death and a resurrection bringing him into a new life in Christ. He commented that the invisible theme of death and resurrection "patterned me on that retreat." From then on this law of death and resurrection, "a living law that shatters us and, by shattering us, also heals us," was "a kind of invisible theme of my life. We know God, the more we are 'in God' and not in ourselves."[13]

To be in God has the characteristics of an ever new "event." It is to find ourselves in the mystery of Triune love where

11. " 'Es stellt sich vor': Hans Urs von Balthasar," *Das neue Buch* (Luzern) 7 (1945), 43.

12. "Pourquoi je me suis fait prêtre," *Editions Centre Diocésain de Documentation* (Tournai, 1959), 19-22, espec. 21-22.

13. "Pourquoi je me suis fait prêtre," 21-22.

relationality, giving and mutuality shape our truest identity. In Jesus Christ, the Son, and with him as our brother, we are projected toward the Father whose word is always love. And the enveloping "atmosphere" of this event is the catholicity of the Spirit's embrace.

Communion

Communion is a central feature of von Balthasar's ecclesiology. He sees the Church as a community that transmits the very communion of life that is God. Furthering communion was also the aim of the projects he pursued so fervently in life. Together with Adrienne von Speyr he set up the Community of Saint John, named after the evangelist who most explicitly highlighted the trinitarian nature of God revealed in Jesus Christ. The name of the international review that he helped to establish was *Communio*. In this chapter we want to briefly examine von Balthasar's writings on how the Church's communion is born.

A Decision Taken in Trinitarian Communion

Von Balthasar considers the logic of communion to be one which shapes all of God's dealings with humankind. The divine plan of salvation reflects the "giving," "receiving" and "uniting" of the inner divine dialogue of love. The very plan to create and redeem was itself "decided upon" in trinitarian decision between the Father, Son and Spirit:

> The Father has created [the world] "in the Son" and for the glorification of the Son; while the Son has both created it and redeemed it for the glory of the Father, in order to lay it perfected at the feet of the Father (1 Cor 15:24-28); and the Spirit transfigures it, not in order to reveal himself, but to reveal to the creation the infinite love between Father and Son, and to bestow on creation the form of this love.[14]

---

14. *Explorations III: Creator Spirit,* 12.

The "atmosphere" in which God decides to create and redeem us is trinitarian, and it is this trinitarian reciprocity which God wants to impress upon creation. The execution of his plan is shaped in the same trinitarian fashion, with each of the three divine Persons participating. The marvel is that creation too is involved. Echoing Karl Barth who writes "God works on us, for us, with us," von Balthasar's writings strive to demonstrate how humanity is taken seriously as God's partner both in the event of redemption and in its preparation.[15] While always respecting the sovereignty of God's action, his writings reflect that what God wants to do *for* us he only does *with* us.

Certainly, God does not "need" us to be himself as Hegel's philosophy suggests. God is everything and he is above all his works (Sir 43:27-38). But a true theology of redemption must steer a course between a radical theo-monism (where it's all God's doing and humanity counts for nothing) and a Promethean human titanism (where human action seems everything). For von Balthasar the key to this is what he calls a "theo-dramatic" framework, where redemption is viewed in terms of a drama involving God and humanity as the main actors. It is a drama that unfolds around the theme of the inter-relationship between the infinite freedom of God and humankind's finite freedom. In the Word made flesh, the co-ordinates of this drama are made clear in terms of communion. In Jesus Christ there is neither confusion nor separation; there is, rather, unity in distinction between humanity and God.[16] This vertical communion establishes the true horizontal co-existence of humankind.

---

15. See *Theo-Drama I*, 8.
16. For studies on von Balthasar's Christology see Hanspeter Heinz, *Der Gott des Je-Mehr: Der christologische Ansatz Hans Urs von Balthasars* (Bern/Frankfurt: Peter Lang, 1975) and Giovanni Marchesi, *La Cristologia di Hans Urs von Balthasar* (Rome: P.U.G., 1977).

The "Great Mystery"

Within the theo-dramatic perspective, von Balthasar reminds us that Jesus Christ is not to be read in an isolated fashion. In his divine-human identity, he is both totally turned toward the Father (and guided by the Spirit) and toward humanity. In sending his Word among us, God chooses to "need" a partner, who will be in a relationship of communion with him and through whom his Word can communicate his trinitarian life to the world. This is the reason for Paul's wonder at the "great mystery" of Christ and the Church (Eph 5:32). Von Balthasar shares this marvel, because it joins together several themes concerning God's relationship with humanity: the creation of man and woman, the relationship between Christ and the Church, the final form of humanity's participation in the life of the triune God.[17]

Taking his lead from this scriptural notion of the "great mystery," von Balthasar notes some features of the conjugal relationship between man and woman which explain why it is the "highest parable" for expressing God's encounter with humanity.[18] Firstly, marital union presupposes two persons who even in their union remain unmixedly persons. Secondly, the physical union which takes place makes them "one flesh," as the child, the fruit of their union, shows externally. Thirdly, the physical opposition of the sexes (representing the opposition of the spiritual persons in the bodily sphere) makes possible their union.

The male's role in the conjugal act is employed as an analogy for God's initiating role in the divine-human encounter. God is external to creation. He is the one who awakens creation's active and fruitful receptivity. Of course, no analogy is completely perfect. Von Balthasar is aware of the limitations and possible misinterpretations involved. Firstly, man, Adam,

---

17. See *Explorations II: Spouse of the Word,* 184ff; *Elucidations,* 105-107.
18. See *The Glory of the Lord VII: Theology: The New Covenant* (Edinburgh: T&T Clark, 1989), 395. For following see, *Theo-Drama III,* 283ff.

is never to be identified with God. The Old Testament itself was clearly aware of this ("I am God and not a man," Nm 23:19; Hos 11:9). The Book of Genesis affirms that man and woman are created in the "image of God," equal in the rank of their free human nature. Secondly, unlike man, God needs no partner to set his fecundity free. Thirdly, it is only an analogy — unlike God's continuous providence, the male's function in the act of procreation is incidental, marginal and transitory in character.

To depict woman as paradigm of creation's responsiveness to God is based on a number of reasons. But first a word of caution. On occasion, application of the man-woman analogy to the relationship between God and humanity has been misinterpreted in a way which denigrates woman to being merely (inferior) matter, which must be passively and inactively "informed" by the (male and superior) active spirit. That, however, is not how von Balthasar presents it. He is too well aware of the true sense of scripture and tradition as well as the new insights gained by modern biology into woman's activity in the conception and bringing to birth of a child.[19]

Among the reasons which make the role of woman in a marital union the paradigm of creation's encounter with God, von Balthasar includes the fact that in the sexual sphere woman's fruitfulness appears more active and explicit than the fruitfulness of man in that she is the principle of common fruitfulness. While woman is directed toward insemination (and as such, in terms of analogy, represents the human openness to God's initiating of our human potential fruitfulness), she has her own responsive fruitfulness.

Woman's fruitfulness goes beyond the merely I–Thou of the husband-wife relationship in her producing something "new." She unites the fecundity of both man and woman in that she receives and bears a new creation; thus she is the "glory" of man (1 Cor 11:7). Beyond highlighting the concreteness of woman by way of pointing to a certain primacy of

---

19. See *New Elucidations*, 213-214; 187-198; "Die Würde der Frau," 346-352.

womanhood in the creaturely realm, von Balthasar comments on a "pivotal finding" of modern genetic research, which speaks of the basic embryonic make-up of all living beings as being primarily feminine![20]

The various features of the marital union which we have mentioned are taken up in divine revelation as a language in which God's self-communication in Christ and our participation in that event may be uttered. The man-woman relationship conveys the unity in distinction of Christ and his bridal body. In his writings, von Balthasar highlights how there is a man-woman polarity running throughout the events of creation and redemption. It is one of mutuality and circularity as summarized in Paul's words: "In the Lord woman is not independent of man nor man of woman; for as woman was made from man, so man is now born of woman. And all things are from God" (1 Cor 11:11-12).[21] We will return to these themes later on.

The Feminine Principle [22]

A feminine principle operative throughout the history of salvation can be traced from the very first pages of the Book of Genesis onward. In fact, von Balthasar sees history's progression toward the definitive encounter with the Word made flesh as a movement in creation and humanity toward gaining a responsive feminine countenance. The more humanity is addressed and hears God's call, the more it takes on this responsive countenance, which is personified in representative fashion, firstly in the history of Israel, then in Mary and the Church.

---

20. See *New Elucidations*, 213. He refers us to Adolf Portmann, "Die biologischen Grundfragen der Typenlehre" *Eranos 1974* (Leiden: Brill, 1977), 449-473.
21. *Theo-Drama II*, 373. Cf. E. Przywara, *Mensch, Typologische Anthropologie I* (Nürnberg: Glock und Lutz, 1958).
22. See "Die Würde der Frau"; *Theo-Drama III*, 283-360.

Von Balthasar notes the apocalyptic visionary, who saw Woman-Sion-Mary-Church-the Holy City as a unity (Rv 11:19-21:1).[23] And on this basis he writes of a corporate-individual personality — "Synagogue-Mary-Church." With this term he wants to convey the whole continuum of the feminine principle in the history of salvation. This collectivity, ultimately personified in Mary, is the responsive "partner" whom God chooses to "need" in the incarnation, the paschal mystery and the founding of the Church.

> The Woman — as Synagogue-Mary-Church — is the inseparable unity of that which makes it possible for the Word of God to take on the being of the world, in virtue of the natural-supernatural fruitfulness given to her. As the active power of receiving all that heaven gives, she is the epitome of creaturely power and dignity; she is what God presupposes as the Creator in order to give the seed of the Word to the world.[24]

His thought on the feminine principle is clearly influenced by various writers — Dante's notion of the eternal feminine,[25] Scheeben's reflections on the "great mystery,"[26] Louis Bouyer and Teilhard de Chardin's notion of the sophiological principle in creation,[27] Russian sophiology found in Soloviev's notion of "catholic integration"[28] and in some respects Barth's biblical anthropology and covenant theology.[29] But, above all, one can also detect Adrienne von Speyr's theology of the sexes.

---

23. See Altfrid Kassing, *Das Verhältnis von Kirche und Maria im 12. Kapitel der Apokalypse* (Düsseldorf: Patmos, 1958).
24. *Short Primer*, 90.
25. See *The Glory of the Lord III: Studies in Theological Style: Lay Styles* (San Francisco: Ignatius Press, 1986), 48ff.
26. *Dogmatik II*, n. 423.
27. Louis Bouyer, *Woman in the Church* (San Francisco: Ignatius Press, 1979), 113-121, and Henri de Lubac's commentary on De Chardin in Pierre Teilhard de Chardin, *Hymne an das Ewig-Weibliche* (Einsiedeln: Johannes Verlag, 1968). See also von Balthasar, *Prüfet Alles, das Gute Behaltet* (Ostfildern: Schwabenverlag AG, 1986), 36.
28. *Glory of the Lord*, 279-352.
29. Karl Barth, *Kirchliche Dogmatik III* (Zurich: EVZ-Verlag, 1950).

Beyond Inner-Worldly Analogy [30]

We said above that in sending his Word among us, God chose to "need" Woman ("Synagogue-Mary-Church") as Christ's "counterpart" and "helper." This Woman, however, is not only the presupposition (as the one who allows it to happen) for Christ's incarnation and paschal mystery, but she proceeds from him as his "fullness" (Eph 1:23). The Woman who is to be Christ's "counterpart" is actually produced through the generative act of Christ.

At this point, von Balthasar admits that all inner-worldly analogy fails. The marriage paradigm has its limits, because a husband encounters his wife as a separate person with a freedom and self-surrender which he does not create. In the case of Christ, the Woman who precedes him and is his "helpmate" is generated as his "bride" by his extraordinary act of self-surrender and generation in the paschal mystery. That is why von Balthasar speaks of the relationship between Christ and the Church or between Christ and Mary as "supra-sexual."

He brings us right back to the logic of the inner life of communion in God. Each of the three divine Persons is "transferred" into the others; each contains the others within himself; and each finds his identity in being totally related to and containing the others. To describe God's mutual love, von Balthasar writes of a "supra-masculinity" and "supra-femininity" in God.[31] Not that he is projecting sexuality into God. But, speaking analogically, he sees the Father (the unoriginated One who generates) as "supra-masculine" vis-à-vis the Son, while the Son (who allows himself to be generated in receptivity) is "supra-feminine" vis-à-vis the Father. In his active co-spiring with the Father of the Spirit, the Son is "supra-masculine" and the Spirit "supra-feminine." True to the trinitarian logic, von Balthasar comments that the Father too can

---

30. See *Theo-Drama III*, 339ff.
31. *Theo-Drama V*, 91; *Explorations IV: Spirit and Institution*, 337-350; "Die Würde der Frau," 349ff.

in some sense be seen as "supra-feminine" inasmuch as he allows himself to be co-determined by those who proceed from him. Von Balthasar continues along this line in his reflection upon the inner-trinitarian relations. But it is sufficient for us to note that it is on the basis of his trinitarian doctrine that he sees in the second divine Person the original model for both human masculinity and femininity in a way that precludes any predominance of one sex over another. In the eternal Son of God the archetypes of both sexes have the same eternity and dignity. In the eternal Son there is a "femininity" and "masculinity" in relation to the Father.[32]

In representing the Father to us, however, the Son is masculine. Reading the paschal mystery, together with the creation account (Eve coming from the side of Adam), in the light of the trinitarian logic, von Balthasar maintains that Christ has the feminine element within him, and it is this which flows from him as his "helpmate" through his death on the cross. She is to be, as it were, his "other self."[33] Von Balthasar reads Eve's extraction from Adam and the Church's coming from Christ as images of the Son's springing from the eternal Father.[34]

The mystical body which comes from Christ is so totally united to him that Christ recognizes himself in her as the fruit of his own generating act:

> Jesus, as the Son of God and in his divine mission, has the whole of humankind in view . . . this being so, must not his human, concentrated form find an echo in a similarly human, concentrated form? Insofar as he is an individual conscious subject, he would thus find a fitting social environment; insofar as he is a man, he would find the "helpmate," the "bride" and the "glory" he can recognize as "flesh of my flesh and bone of my bone." However, all this takes place at a level that en-

---

32. See Claudio Giuliodori, *Intelligenza teologica del maschile e del femminile: problemi e prospettive nella rilettura di von Balthasar e P. Evokimov* (Rome: Città Nuova, 1991).
33. See *Explorations II: Spouse of the Word*, 71.
34. "Die Würde der Frau," 348-349.

folds but essentially transcends the proportions of creation because, since he is *God's* Son, his complement and partner can only come forth from his own substance.[35]

This "helper" is, in a sense, "another Christ." As his mystical body, she is in communion with him, but she has also her own distinct identity. All of humanity is potentially this mystical body. "Christ loved the Church and gave himself up for her, that he might sanctify her, having cleansed her by the washing of water with the word, that he might present the Church to himself in splendor, without spot or wrinkle or any such thing, that she might be wholly and without blemish" (Eph 5:25-27). This mystical body of believers continues with Christ his mission of unifying and reconciling all of creation with God (2 Cor 5:19):

> All the same, while this complement and partner comes from him and can thus be called his ("mystical") Body . . . it is not enough for him to see in her *only himself,* an effect of his influence, his work. For he *needs* the one who has come into existence from within him: She is to be his "helpmate" for his work; when he is no longer on earth as an historical person, she will represent him and continue his work.[36]

Once again the trinitarian exchange of love is the horizon. The greatness of God's relationship with creation is that in Christ he has brought created reality to enjoy free partnership with him. God has, in a sense, raised us through grace to his level. Through the work of the Creator Holy Spirit, the bond of unity in the Trinity, creation has in Christ been set into the bosom of the Father, sharing in the divine dialogue of love.

---

35. *Theo-Drama III*, 341.
36. *Theo-Drama III*, 341.

The Church as "Body-Bride" of Christ

From what we have seen in this section so far, we can begin to appreciate why the statement "the Church is a community" is not for von Balthasar primarily a sociological declaration but rather a theological affirmation.[37] In other words, he doesn't see the Church as a community built on mere memory of Christ or as a social project based on his teaching.

What is primary in the Church is that the new community brought about by the life, death and resurrection of Jesus Christ is an active sharing in *the* community of communities, the life of the Triune God. In order to keep before our eyes the notion of the Church's communion coming totally from the Word made flesh, von Balthasar couples two Pauline images of the Church, namely, the "body" and "bride." He writes of the Church in terms of the "Body-Bride" of Christ, and he names it with a term which Adrienne von Speyr also favored: "Mary-Church."[38]

On the one hand, in von Balthasar's view, the body image highlights the eucharistic-sacramental mediation of the trinitarian life, poured out through the dying Christ into the Church. This is symbolized in the blood and water flowing from his side. The body image presents the Church as an extension, a communication, and a partaking of the personality of Christ in external sacramental forms.

On the other hand, the bride image affirms the contradistinct openness and response of love to Christ the bridegroom and head of the Church. It refers to that feminine element of the "supra-sexual" relationship between Christ and the Church. Through the outpouring of the Spirit, the Church stands vis-à-vis Christ as a "someone," a subject, a person, a co-operating agent formed by the subjectivity and

---

37. Von Balthasar refers us to Y. Congar's good summary of various speculative attempts to describe the identity of the Church, "La personne, 'L'église' " *Revue Thomiste* 71 (1971), 613-640.
38. See *Theo-Drama III*, 351ff; *Explorations II: Spouse of the Word*, 157ff; B. Albrecht, *Eine Theologie des Katholischen II*, 166-167.

personalities of all who form the Church. This is personified in Mary, who is clothed in virginity, spousal responsiveness and maternity.

Mission

Peter Henrici has written that had the students who came into contact with von Balthasar during his days as a student chaplain in Basel been asked for a description of his thought, they would undoubtedly have cited "mission" as a key word in it.[39] Von Balthasar's view of the Church's mission is vast, because its dimensions are nothing less than Christ's bridging mission which embraces everyone (Col 1:28) and the whole cosmos (2 Cor 5:19). Christ's mission is to build up his kingdom, form humanity into a family, restore paradise. In a word, he wants to share his trinitarian life of communion.

Christ will only do this *with* us. His work, therefore, is not something external to the Church. And neither is the Church's mission some mere activity she has to do apart from Christ. In von Balthasar's writings, her mission and her nature as communion are intimately linked, since what passes over from Jesus Christ to the Church is "the entire trinitarian life in course of communication." In him and with him, the Church is the vehicle of this life reaching into creation, the world and history.[40] Trinity, Christology and Church (and therefore also Church mission) form an inseparable whole.[41]

Von Balthasar's theology of mission is rooted in the relations of the Trinity. He defines Christ's personhood in terms of mission as an extension or external icon of the internal procession of the Son from the Father. While, in some respects, this section on mission seems to appropriate mission to the Holy Spirit, we shall also be alert to the fact that in von Balthasar's theology each of the three divine Persons is, in a certain sense, defined in terms of mission. Not least because it

---

39. Henrici, "Hans Urs von Balthasar," 32.
40. *Explorations II: Spouse of the Word*, 183; *Theo-Drama III*, 340ff.
41. *Elucidations*, 79; *Theo-Drama II*, 309; *Explorations II: Spouse of the Word*, 184ff.

is the very unity of the divine Being that is the source and summit of all its missionary dynamics.

The Shape of the Church

The "Body-Bride" which has emerged from Christ is charity, reflecting the divine triune life of love which has been poured out in Jesus Christ and in which she has been fashioned.[42] In his personalist ecclesiology, von Balthasar wants to express the implications of this for the concrete shape of the Church. Christ's Body-Bride is not a monolithic block. Just as there are three Persons in the one God, so too the Church is a dynamic multi-dimensional reality made up of various "person-principles" who form one mystical body-bride of Christ.[43]

We have already referred to von Balthasar's writings on the key figures who surrounded Jesus during his life such as Mary, Peter, the apostles, John the Baptist, Martha and Mary. "The Risen Lord," he comments, "who wills to be present in his Church all days to the end of time, cannot be isolated from the 'constellation' of his historical life."[44] It was through each person's self-surrender in his or her mission that the Church-community is formed. This was true of the founding moment in the Church, and it is still true today.

Accordingly, the Church is not to be seen as an extra-personal principle of unity beside and above the unity of persons but, in Christ, she is formed from the "surrendered unities" of each one of us. Once again, von Balthasar points to the unity of God's nature, which is not something in addition to the interplay of relations between the divine Persons.[45]

---

42. See "The Church as 'Caritas'" *Elucidations*, 245-266.
43. See Antonio Sicari, "Mary, Peter and John: Figures of the Church," *Communio* 19 (1992), 189-207.
44. *Office of Peter*, 162.
45. *Theo-Drama III*, 416.

The key to all of this is the Holy Spirit, the Church's inner-most ground, the third divine Person to whom the building and extension of the Church has been entrusted by Jesus. Through the outpouring of the Spirit, the individuals who surrounded Jesus during his life were not absorbed through their election, call and mission in the risen Christ. On the contrary, the ray of grace which bestowed a mission upon them extended their ray of action beyond a merely personal fruitfulness to the dimensions of the fruitfulness of the entire mystical body of Christ:

> For the Church is not one person among others; nor is she a supra-personal institution, what is left once all the human beings have been abstracted from a human community, namely, the framework, the statutes and the customs. Nor is she merely a kind of impersonal sap arising from the roots into the branches; the analogy of the subhuman, organic life illustrates only one aspect, at most, of the Church's unity, and not the most significant at that. The Church's unity of life comes about through the self-emptying and externalizing of God's unique spirit-life *beyond, in* and *through* the individuals integrated in it. Their creaturely uniqueness is not limited nor endangered but rather, on the contrary, by grace it is put in touch with the uniqueness of God and thus opened to perfection. Everyone who encounters God in faith and love is illuminated by the radiance of the divine uniqueness which comes from the Word and in this radiance the individual is made a member of the one Bride, the Church.[46]

The Holy Spirit unites us as the body of Christ in a way that makes of us a bride before God. The One who is the divine "co-incidence of opposites" (between Father and Son), as von Balthasar calls him, is the bond of unity in distinction of the

---

46. *Prayer*, 93-94.

various members of the Church.[47] In his work of building and
extending the Church as the body of Christ, whose countenance is bridal, the Spirit brings about the mutual-indwelling
(*perichòresis*[48]) of various profiles or principles in the Church.

As we shall see later, it is when they are united in mutual
love that the face of the Church is a Marian transparency to
Christ. This is what enables the Church to act as a magnet
drawing humanity toward the One who is the way, the truth
and the life.

Principles which Remain in the Church

Basing his reflection upon the early developing Church's experience, von Balthasar writes of a basic fourfold structure of
principles in the Church: Petrine, Pauline, Johannine, and
Jacobine. He sees the Marian as the all-embracing principle. In
writing about these principles, he wants to convey that the archetypal experience of faith of each of these paradigmatic believers continues in the life of the Church with specific characteristics. Let's look briefly at some of their main traits:[49]

The Petrine principle is the most obvious. It recalls the figure
of Peter. From his reading of the Gospels, the Acts of the Apostles and Peter's letters, von Balthasar views Peter as concerned
with the proclamation of the kerygma and its concrete realization in Christian life. Peter's continuing mission has to do with
the creed being preached in a structured manner throughout
the world through the pastoral office. It is the hierarchical, institutional dimension of the Church representing the "objective" dimension of sanctity. We will return to this later.

The Pauline principle is linked with the missionary character
of Paul, the apostle to the Gentiles, the one who became a
Christian by pure grace, without works and merits and

---

47. *Explorations II: Spouse of the Word,* 191.
48. *Office of Peter,* 145.
49. See *Glory of the Lord I,* 352-364; *Office of Peter,* 136-222, 308-330; *Explorations II: Spouse of the Word,* 157ff.

relentlessly broke with the past. Paul's continuing mission can be seen in the dimension of the ever new and unforeseen vertical irruption of new charisms in the history of the Church. It is a prophetic-heavenly principle. Involved here are the great missionary charisms, the great conversions, the great visions poured out over the Church in words inspired by the Spirit. The emphasis is on the vertical extension and structure of the Church. The great charisms derive from the "Jerusalem above" and are witnessed to in word and life. Hence, freedom in the Holy Spirit is highlighted, although submission to Peter is a sign of the authenticity of the missions. The Pauline tradition infuses vision and certainty of salvation into the Church through its charismatic dimension.

The Johannine principle is one in which von Balthasar sees reflected so much of his own work. John is the beloved disciple, the evangelist of the new commandment. Von Balthasar considers John's continuing mission as one of unity. It synthesizes the Petrine and Pauline elements and combines them with contemplative vision. This dimension of the Church is embodied in all those endowed with special charisms, those who live the evangelical counsels and those whose mission is one of contemplative love. They communicate the message that in love everything is possible. So there is also a prophetic-apocalyptic dimension present here. Von Balthasar closely links John with Mary to a degree that in his writings the Marian and Johannine principles are not always easy to distinguish. We shall return to this as well.

The Jacobine principle is based on James, brother of the Lord, who seems to have taken Peter's place after the latter left Jerusalem (Acts 12:17). At the Council of the Apostles, he put forward the decisive motion of reconciliation between Jewish and Gentile Christians (Acts 15:13-21). Above all, however, he represents continuity between the Old and New Covenants, tradition, the legitimacy of the letter of the law as against the mere spirit. James' continuing mission in the Church is the least elaborated upon by von Balthasar. It is that dimension of the Church which affirms the historical sense of things,

continuity, tradition, canon law. Perhaps we could see this
principle embodied in those who caution us against too rapid a
shift in the customs, norms, and traditions of the Church.
Those who search for the "historical" Jesus might be num-
bered among the Jacobine principle as well. It might not be
wrong to mention in this context too those involved in Jew-
ish-Christian dialogue, because they keep before us the origins
of our Christian story.

The Marian Principle

Finally, the Marian principle in the Church. Mary personifies the Church in two ways. Firstly, the whole countenance of
the Church is a Marian transparency to Christ. Secondly, as
the mother who generated the Word from which the Church is
born, and as the bride who co-operates with Christ in the event
of redemption, Mary is the all-embracing principle of the
Church, the point where all the other profiles of the Church
find their fundamental point of internal unity.[50]

Von Balthasar draws particular attention to the interplay
between the Marian and Petrine principles. He sees them as
two co-extensive profiles of the Church around which the
whole of the Church's life revolves. Their interaction is intimately linked with the Church's own identity as a "unity of
two," Christ and his Bride, which we have looked at in this
chapter. If Peter is the point of external unity, the missionary
communion of the Church finds her more fundamental internal point of unity in her Marian archetype and Marian personal center.[51] We shall be returning to this in part four.

Mary, of course, is neither to be reduced to some abstract
principle, nor dissolved into ecclesiology as Laurentin feared
happens in von Balthasar's writings.[52] To avoid this danger,

---

50. *Theo-Drama III*, 352.
51. *Explorations II: Spouse of the Word*, 161; *Glory of the Lord I*, 362; *Theo-Drama III*, 352.
52. "Bulletin sur la Vierge Marie," *Rev. Sc. ph. th.* 58 (1974), 277-328, espec. 279-280.

von Balthasar concedes priority of exposition to Mariology over ecclesiology in his *Theo-drama*.[53] In doing so, however, he doesn't simply want to focus on Marian privileges in isolation. No one, he comments, pays less attention to her personal "privileges" than the mother of Christ. She enjoys these "only insofar as they are shared in by all of her children in the Church."[54] Taking our cue from his own exposition in the *Theo-Drama* before moving on to a fuller treatment of the Marian principle in the Church, we shall now turn our attention to the salient features of Mary's own personal role in the event of the Word coming to dwell among us.

---

53. See *Theo-Drama III*, 291.
54. *Elucidations*, 111.

Part 3

Mary for Today

"Mary is woman, pure and simple, in whom everything feminine in salvation history is summed up."[1] These words summarize the richness, simplicity and beauty of Mary as portrayed by von Balthasar in his writings. Of all the women spoken of in scripture, Mary is the one who receives the greatest range of attention. She is the woman most spoken of in scripture. In all of history, he comments, nothing is more eloquent than the whole pattern of Mary's life, because each of her life situations is history at its most fulfilled. While theologians, preachers and hymnologists may try to express her identity in concepts and lyrics, von Balthasar considers Mary a holy, public mystery, indeed a "secret."[2]

In saying all of this, his intention is certainly not to remove Mary from us, as is further stressed by the title of one of his works, *Mary for Today*. Rather, he proposes her as a model of discipleship because of the characteristics of her "journey" in faith. In fact, as a pilgrim she found faith even more difficult than we do. Even the "legitimate demands of feminism" can appeal to Mary as model.[3]

Peelman has written that von Balthasar does not stress an elaborate Mariology but rather one which concentrates on the essential.[4] His writings contemplate the twelve gospel

---

1. "Our Lady in Monasticism," 52-56, espec. 52.
2. "Heilig öffentlich Geheimnis" 1-12; "Maria in der kirchlichen Lehre und Frömmigkeit" in Joseph Ratzinger and Hans Urs von Balthasar, *Maria-Kirche im Ursprung* (Freiburg im Breisgau: Herder, 1980), 41-79.
3. "Maria nel nostro tempo," *Nuovo Areopago* (Rome) 6 (1987), 68-71, espec. 68.
4. Achiel Peelman, "L'ésprit et Marie dans L'Oeuvre Théologique de Hans Urs von Balthasar," *Science et ésprit* 30 (1978), 279-294, espec. 291.

mysteries of Mary: the annunciation (Lk 1:26-38); the pregnancy (Lk 1 and Mt 1); the visit to Elizabeth and the Baptist,
the Magnificat (Lk 1:39-56); the birth of our Lord (Mt 2:1-12;
Lk 2:1-20); the presentation in the Temple (Lk 2:21-40); the
flight into Egypt (Mt 2:13-23); the finding of the child in the
Temple (Lk 2:41-52); the wedding in Cana (Jn 2:1-11); the rebuff of Mary and the brothers (Mt 12:46-50; Mk 3:31-35; Lk
8:19-21); the blessing of the believers (Lk 11:28); Mary beneath the cross (Jn 19:25-28); Mary praying with the Church
(Acts 1:14).[5]

Viewing these gospel scenes as a "hall of mirrors," he depicts
Mary in a network of relationships and connections — with
the Father, with Jesus, with the Spirit, with Eve, with the people of Israel, with the Church, with humanity. He also compares these gospel scenes to "stars" in the sky and writes:
"They demand to be seen as a constellation, and they become
brighter and deeper the closer they are brought together."[6] By
way of example, he mentions that the "sword" prophecy in
Luke (Lk 2:35) clearly points to the scene at the cross as depicted in John's gospel (Jn 19:25-27); and "the Spirit" and the
"power of the Most High" that comes upon Mary in the annunciation (Lk 1:35) points to the "Spirit" and the "power
from on high" that comes upon the Church in the risen Christ
and at Pentecost (Lk 24:49 and Acts 1:8).

Through meditating upon all of these mysteries and their
mutual inter-relating, we come to glimpse Mary's "form" (a favorite notion used in von Balthasar's writings to refer to the totality which shines through over and beyond all the individual
elements). But two mysteries in particular are central — her
yes at the annunciation and the renewed yes at the foot of the
cross. Both these scenes epitomize the fundamental feature of
her life — freedom. Mary is a paradigm of the freedom which is
realized when we let God speak his word in our lives and give
us a mission in the world.

---

5. *Theo-Drama III*, 299; *Theologie der Geschichte* (Einsiedeln: Johannes Verlag, 1959), 91. See
also Adrienne von Speyr, *Handmaid of the Lord*.
6. *Theo-Drama III*, 299.

The longest and deepest piece of von Balthasar's writings on Mary appears in the *Theo-Drama,* a work dedicated to the dramatic encounter between infinite and finite freedom. Trinitarian and Christological motifs abound. Any reflection on Mary's role must proceed, therefore, against the background of the Christological and trinitarian truths that we have introduced in the previous part around the leitmotifs of mystery, communion and mission. Mary's origin is within the *mystery.* She is woman of *communion.* Her *mission* continues between time and eternity.

Mary, Woman Whose Home Is
in the Mystery

To say that Mary's "home" is in the mystery is to say that the unique design God has for Mary originates within the trinitarian dialogue of love that "decided" on creation and redemption. Her origins are in God's eternal plan of salvation. Contemporaneous with the Son's offer of himself to the Father, and the Father's acceptance and mandate of the Son, and with the Spirit's readiness to mediate between heaven and earth, God included Mary's word of assent as an indispensable part of his plan to unite all things under Christ (Eph 1:10; cf. Jn 17). From the outset, Mary's word of assent was, therefore, the echo, the reverberation of the eternal word of assent, which the Son gave in heaven to the Father's trinitarian plan of salvation.

Mary was "chosen before the foundation of the world" to be the Savior's mother, "to be holy and immaculate before him." Not only was Mary chosen as mother, she was also chosen to correspond to the Son and be presented by him to himself as that "bride" who would conclude in advance for all, and in all, the love contract between God and the world, between the eternal and the created heart.[7]

Von Balthasar traces the first scriptural reference to Mary to the primordial good news contained in Genesis 3:15.[8] This is the passage following the Fall where God promises a liberating future for humanity. Following both exegetical studies and the light of tradition since the early Church Fathers (especially in writings based on the Vulgate edition of the Bible), von

---

7. *Man in History*, 75.
8. He refers us to A. Feuillet, "Der Sieg der Frau nach dem Protoevangelium," *Internationale Katholische Zeitschrift Communio* 7 (1978), 26-35.

Balthasar considers the woman spoken of in this passage to be Mary:

> In banishing man from paradise, God did not con-
> demn him to despair. At the entrance to the Garden of
> Eden he placed the flaming sword that bore the like-
> ness of Mother and child. A woman would come who
> would turn Eve's curse into a blessing. In the full obe-
> dience of her assent, she would extinguish what Eve's
> greedy disobedience had kindled. In the flawless pu-
> rity of her perpetual virginity, she would realize — and
> more than realize — the fecundity of paradise by bear-
> ing God himself, who would redeem the world from its
> guilt. In the perfect poverty that put her whole being,
> body and soul, at the disposal of God's design, she
> would replace with the riches of man's original self-
> giving the poverty of need he was compelled to endure
> in his fallen state. She would not accomplish this by
> her own strength and virtue, but as the chosen one, as
> the one supported by God's grace, more encompassed
> by this grace than Adam and Eve had ever been.[9]

Mary emerges right at the beginning of our sacred history, therefore, at the departure from paradise. We meet her in the little house of Nazareth.

A Gift from God's Treasure-House

As one of us, Mary is to be mother of the Savior. In solidarity with us, she is to "help" her Son. To carry out this particular role, Mary has to be unique, and indeed she is. Fashioned by God as a creature, she is rooted in paradise. Von Balthasar admiringly refers to Péguy's poetic acclaim of this in his six great *Chartres* poems. From the fallen temporal order to the pres-

---

9. *Christian State of Life*, 122.

ence of unfallen time, Péguy appeals to the holiness of Mary.[10] As "a genuine citadel of compassion" Mary's uniqueness lies in the fact that she lives "between paradise and the Fall."

One of the doctrines expressing this is the Immaculate Conception, a doctrine which took centuries (especially from Scotus onward) to grasp fully. Von Balthasar's presentation of this doctrine could be described as a Catholic version of the reformers' *sola gratia*,[11] because he writes of it as a gift from the triune God's treasure-house of love.

Because of the Fall, humanity was locked in an inability to love Love. When the *summum* of love was to be poured into the darkness of creation it needed love to accept this Love. How could this be in our fallen condition? A liberating gift from the heavenly treasure-house was needed to let this happen in a way that respected our freedom. Mary's pre-redemption was this gift. As a gift from the Father to the Son in the Spirit, Mary's sinlessness was the ultimate prerequisite of the incarnation by which the Son could offer himself, along with us, in the Spirit to the Father.

While the Immaculate Conception is certainly a personal privilege, it was a gift granted to Mary in view of the universality or catholicity of her yes, which enabled the Father to generate his Word in our world. She was able to say a limitless yes. It also enabled Mary to be the mother who was able to mediate in requisite purity everything human her child needed.

Mary's immaculate conception certainly does not remove her from us. On the contrary, von Balthasar's eminently positive presentation points to quite the opposite. When we consider that sin isolates and thwarts effective solidarity, we realize that rather than removing Mary from solidarity with us (and this fear caused centuries of delay in its formulation), the doctrine of the Immaculate Conception speaks of her love, solidarity, closeness and oneness with us. Precisely because she stands "outside" the fallen world in an innocence like that of

10. See *Glory of the Lord III: Lay Styles* (San Francisco: Ignatius Press, 1986), 400-517, espec. 413, 479ff.
11. See Hanspeter Heinz, "Maria als Ort der Begegnung," 137.

Adam and Eve before the Fall, she can love in a uniquely perfect manner.[12]

This explains why, in his homilies, von Balthasar speaks of the Immaculate Conception of Mary in terms of the abolition of barriers.[13] The cloak of the Immaculate Mary envelops the divisions, oppositions and failures of this world, because in her God's reconciling and unifying plan for humankind is clearly evident. Though immersed in the wounded condition of our fallen nature, she is paradise restored.

---

12. *Christian State of Life,* 206.
13. *You Crown the Year with Your Goodness* (San Francisco: Ignatius Press, 1984), 264-269.

Mary, Woman of Communion

"When I get to heaven, I shall walk up to Mary . . . and say, 'well done sister'!"[14] This remark, allegedly made by von Balthasar to Karl Barth, is a pen-picture of his admiration for Mary's active, vibrant role in what he calls the theodramatic action of our redemption. Mary is center stage in the drama of redemption as a woman of communion — communion with God above all but also with the people of the Old Testament and with the family of the New Testament. Rooted in the history of God's first covenant with his people, she is a meeting-point with the new covenant in Jesus Christ.

This chapter aims to present some of the features of how Mary was this woman of communion throughout her whole life. In embodying the tension of transition from one covenant to the other, Mary's life was shaped by God. The transition that occurs and in which she plays a central role is not the result of "works" but of a grace, a miracle.[15]

At the outset of this chapter on Mary as a woman of communion, it is good to recall one of the earliest aspects of her life to be highlighted in the prayer of the Church, namely, her virginity.[16] It speaks of the novelty of the miracle-transition that comes about through her. On the one hand, in her virginity Israel's hopeful faith and obedience is both bodily and spiritually concretized and personalized. On the other hand, this virginity is a novelty that flowers with the coming of Jesus Christ and is totally directed toward the life of communion that emerges in him.

---

14. See Paul S. Fiddes, "Mary in the Theology of Karl Barth" in Alberic Stacpoole (ed.), *Mary in Doctrine and Devotion: Papers of the Liverpool Congress, 1989, of the Ecumenical Society of the Blessed Virgin Mary* (Dublin: Columba Press, 1990), 111-126, espec. 124.
15. *Theo-Drama III*, 328ff.
16. See, for instance, Ignatius of Antioch, *To the Ephesians* 7, 2.

Mary's conception of the child Jesus was not simply another instance in the row of divine interventions in favor of sterile women that we find recounted throughout the Old Testament, beginning with Sarah and continuing right up to Elizabeth. God's intervention in Mary's case signals a novelty. There is no human father. It is exclusively the Holy Spirit who overshadows the virgin so that the One to whom she is to give birth can be called "Son of the Most High." He is Son of the eternal Father. Her virginity is directed toward divine maternity.[17] Her child is to bring God who is love and eternal life into the world.

On this basis, proceeding almost as a Church Father along with Ephraem, Andrew of Crete and John Damascene, von Balthasar sees Mary's virginity as marking a new kind of generation in history, one which surpasses the physical generation of children born into the cycle of human birth, life and death. With the coming of Christ a "new creation" opens up, the "cosmos" of Christ, which is a life "from above," one which will never end.

Shaped by faith, hope and love, Mary's virginity is a sign of this new "cosmos" and its fruitfulness. Taking her stand and finding her fulfillment in God alone, she is a sign of the original fruitful state of paradise, which is restored in her. Paradoxically, what we see in Mary's virginity is the highest instance of human fruitfulness.[18] It is a reflection of the fruitfulness of the divine triune life that has shaped her identity.

There is a virginal element in the mutual love of the three divine Persons. And Mary's virginity reflects this also in her married state. The doctrine of her virginity is, in fact, not at all intended to denigrate marriage. Mary marries Joseph. But her abiding physical virginity is the bodily dimension of her abiding inner virginity. This is necessary both for the incarnation

---

17. See "Empfangen durch den Heiligen Geist, geboren von der Jungfrau Maria," in W. Sandfuchs, *Ich glaube: Vierzehn Betrachtungen zum Apostolischen Glaubensbekenntnis* (Würzburg: Echter Verlag, 1975), 39-49; "Maria in der kirchlichen Lehre," 50-51; *Christian State of Life*, 201ff.
18. *In the Fullness of Faith*, 2.

where she is to become Mother of God and for the paschal mystery where, in what von Balthasar calls a "supra-sexual" relationship, she is to become bride of Christ.

The garment of inner virginity is what is truly essential. In her nothingness and impossibility as virgin, she hands everything over to God, and also expects everything from him. Ultimately, this is the inner form of all Christian life.

Mary's bodily virginity expresses her faith, her total, active yes to God. Augustine said of Mary that she conceived in her mind first before conceiving in her body *(prius concepit mente quam ventre)*. Her whole being, from the apex of her spirit to the depths of her unconscious self was a continuous yes to God. Once again, von Balthasar's writings on Mary's virginal faith can be considered a Catholic version of the Reformers' *sola fide*.[19]

Mary, the Prophetess

Jesus Christ was not an isolated entity without historical connections, dropping from heaven, as it were, like a single meteorite.[20] A history was prepared for him, one that would welcome him, nurture him, but one that he who came "from above" would also fulfill from within. As we saw in the last section, the decision to redeem us was a trinitarian one. So too was the preparation and execution of that plan in history.

In God the Father's plan, the welcoming history prepared for Jesus is summarized in Mary. Taking his lead from Laurentin's exegetical analysis of Luke's Infancy Narratives with their mosaic of Old Testament references, von Balthasar applies the Daughter of Sion motif (Zep 3:14) to Mary. It is a title that links her with Jerusalem and the holy remnant after the exile, expecting God's promises of salvation.[21] She

---

19. Cf. Hanspeter Heinz, "Maria als Ort der Begegnung," 137.
20. *Short Primer*, 88.
21. *Glory of the Lord VII*, 8-69. Cf. René Laurentin, *Structure et Théologie de Luc I-II* (Paris, 1957).

summarizes the history of Israel as the expectant environment into which Jesus is to be born.

Gregory I (540-604) regarded Mary as the personification of the Synagogue, the people who have come together in expectation of the Messiah.[22] At the daybreak of the fulfillment of Israel's history, she recalls and represents the *anawim,* the poor, the powerless and the humble for whom God, through the mouths of the prophets, demands physical and social as well as spiritual justice (Am 2:6; Is 3:15; 10:2, etc). Von Balthasar stretches this theme of expectancy and, together with the early Church writers and Rupert of Deutz,[23] views Mary as the prophetess of the Old Testament, glimpsed at various points of Israel's history:

> Thus just like Christ, Mary too is coming throughout the Old Covenant. The Fathers see her prefigured in varied ways — in the true "Daughter of Sion," in the thorn-bush that was burned but not consumed, in the Ark of the Covenant, in Isaiah's "shoot," in the *shekinah* cloud, in Ezekiel's closed door through which no one but the Lord can pass, in the closed garden and the sealed spring of the Song of Songs. . . . This view is justified by the many Old Testament passages and symbols quoted by Luke himself in his infancy narratives in order to show how they are fulfilled in Jesus and Mary. It explains the Fathers' fondnesss for describing Mary as the fulfillment of Old Testament prophecy, as the *prophetissa'.*[24]

Making her own the personal cry of entire generations crying out for redemption: "Oh, that thou wouldst rend the heavens and come down" (Is 63:19), Mary is the meeting point of prophecy and wisdom which descends from on high. Speaking

---

22. *Hom. 3, I in Evang.* (PL 76, 1086). See *Theo-Drama III,* 329.
23. *De operibus Spiritus Sancti,* 9 (PL 167:1578).
24. *Theo-Drama III,* 328. See also *Who is a Christian,* 71-75.

through the prophets, the Spirit is the active one who has prepared the terrain. And it is in Mary that all roads meet.[25]

Mary's Yes, the Holy Spirit and the Trinity

Von Balthasar doesn't believe in the tradition which says that as a young girl Mary made a private vow to remain a virgin. Such an action would have run counter to the motherhood that Jewish girls would have desired precisely as a sign of God's blessing and a hope of participation in the future coming of the Messiah. Mary lives as a child of God the Father. She wants neither virginity nor marriage but simply seeks to do God's unique will for her.

However, Mary's childlike abandonment to whatever God wants can in some way be seen as that inner virginity spoken of above. Mary does not reflect on herself but rests in her Lord (Lk 1:48) and gives herself over to him. She trusts in the Father. And living as a child of the Father she learns from the Holy Spirit. Von Balthasar remarks that by looking at Mary we can learn much about the fruitfulness of living as a child of the Father.[26]

Although she lived with an attitude of constant expectancy, the annunciation presented her with an unimagined novelty. The voice from heaven (*bat qol*) which introduced Mary into her calling and mission was like a "lightning-bolt," a miracle that had absolutely no counterpart in her human experience. How could it be otherwise when we consider that the annunciation begins a uniquely new journey in history, with Christ coming from the bosom (*Schoß*) of the eternal Father to the womb (*Schoß*) of the temporal mother.[27]

---

25. *Glory of the Lord I*, 338. Cf. John Macquarrie, "Immaculate Conception" *Communio* 7 (1980), 100-112, espec. 103.
26. See *Wenn ihr nicht werdet wie dieses Kind*, 55. See also Gustav Siewerth, *Metaphysik der Kindheit* (Einsiedeln: Johannes Verlag, 1957).
27. *Threefold Garland*, 30.

Mary stands alone before God, and her great response is yes. "Behold I am the handmaid of the Lord. Let what you have said be done unto me" (Lk 1:38). Her yes is, as we have just seen, fashioned in advance as a gift from God's treasure-house. It is a yes of communion. Through the work of the Spirit, Mary's pre-redemption in Jesus Christ ensured a yes of love, which would adequately respond to God the Father. Indeed, her yes echoes the Son's obedience to the Father ("Here I am, I come to do your will," Heb 10:7) in carrying out his mission.

Mary calls herself a servant (of the Lord and of the Spirit) even when she is addressed by the angel with the honor due to a queen. Her yes is to all that may lie in God's word and will. It is a moment of maximum activity, a vibrant readiness of love, involving all her human powers and energies. Here now is the all-embracing vow within which occurs the miracle of motherhood.

It would be difficult to exaggerate the centrality of the annunciation theme in von Balthasar's overall theological framework. Throughout his writings he refers repeatedly to the Holy Spirit's overshadowing of Mary.[28] In sending us his Son, the Father's great love enters into the world and history as an "event" brought about by the Holy Spirit. It is in this event that Mary becomes a living tabernacle.

There are two major points that von Balthasar draws out from the scene of the annunciation. Firstly, and above all, he sees in it the first explicit revelation of God's triune life. The angel announced to Mary not just the incarnation but fundamentally the entire mystery of the Trinity.[29]

The angel's declaration which we find in the first chapter of Luke's gospel is threefold: "Hail Mary, full of grace, the Lord (i.e., the *Father* is with you! . . . You will conceive in your womb

---

28. Some examples: *Glory of the Lord* II, 60ff; *Theo-Drama III*, 183ff, *Theo-Drama V*, 464, *Theologik III*, 42-44, 260, 261; *Man in History*, 74; *Christian State of Life*, 201; *Explorations II: Spouse of the Word*, 162; *Explorations III: Creator Spirit*, 118, 123.

29. *Mary for Today*, 35; *Theologik III*, 44ff, 220; *Prayer*, 193-195; "Maria in der kirchlichen Lehre," 51-52. See also Von Speyr, *Handmaid of the Lord*, 28-34.

and bear a *Son* and you shall call his name Jesus. . . . The *Holy Spirit* will come upon you and . . . overshadow you." This new opening of the heavens reveals a threefold life in God.

Moreover, von Balthasar stresses the notion of a "trinitarian inversion" which takes place in the incarnation.[30] With the incarnation there is a reversal of the inner-divine relationship between the Son and the Spirit. Influenced by Sergius Bulgakow, he employs this notion of a trinitarian inversion to describe how, in the incarnation, the Son empties himself out of obedience to the Father and allows the Spirit to take the lead. He becomes man through the Spirit. During his public ministry he is guided in his mission by the Spirit who represents the Father's will to him as an objective rule which he must obey. The Spirit exists in and over Jesus until his death. Then, through his death and resurrection, the order reverts and the Spirit flows forth from the Son to the Father as well as to the Church and the world.

The second significant aspect of the scene of the annunciation is what it tells us about Mary's link with the Spirit. While von Balthasar himself dealt explicitly with the link between Mary and the Holy Spirit in only one of his articles, others such as Achiel Peelman, T'Joen and Sachs have drawn our attention to the importance of this theme in his writings.[31] One of his favorite images for Mary is, in fact, "Vessel of the Holy Spirit."[32] Admittedly, as Tossou comments, the reader remains disappointed that he didn't develop his thought on Mary's experience of the Spirit. Von Balthasar's view, however, is that since the Holy Spirit is the most mysterious of the three divine Persons, his relationship with Mary is difficult to

---

30. *Theo-Drama III*, 183ff; *Christian State of Life*, 191; *Explorations IV: Spirit and Institution*, 231ff; *Theologik III*, 28-31; 41-45; 166-168. Cf. Mauro Jöhri, *Descensus Dei: Teologia della Croce nell'opera di Hans Urs von Balthasar* (Rome: P.U.L., 1981), 275-278, 363-365. See also Sergius Bulgakow, *Le Paraclet* (Paris: Aubier, 1946), 237.

31. Von Balthasar, "Maria und der Geist," 173-177; Achiel Peelman, "L'ésprit et Marie"; Michel T'Joen, *Marie et l'ésprit dans la théologie de Hans Urs von Balthasar* (Louvain-La-Neuve, unpublished doctoral thesis, 1988), 164; John Sachs, *Spirit and Life: The Pneumatology and Christian Spirituality of Hans Urs von Balthasar* (Tübingen: University Press, 1984), espec. 243-247.

32. See *Elucidations*, 95; *Office of Peter*, 208; *Threefold Garland*, 125.

clarify.[33] In any case, he repeatedly refers to the Holy Spirit coming upon Mary at the annunciation.

He comments that through the conception of the Son by the Holy Spirit in the Virgin's womb, the third Person of the Trinity is himself touched in a way analogous to the incarnation of the Son and gains a particular contact with humanity; in this way the Spirit explores the furthest depths of human liberty.[34] No matter how much he links the Spirit with Mary at the annunciation, however, von Balthasar is careful not to fall into a false exaggeration. Commenting upon L. Boff's Mariology, he praises much of it that is beautiful and in agreement with tradition but questions his contention that Mary was overshadowed by the Holy Spirit in such a way that she can and must be described as hypostatically united with the Spirit. He suggests that Boff refer more to Teilhard de Chardin and Louis Bouyer, who are close to Boff's basic intention but develop their thought in an orthodox form.[35] He goes on to say that because of his human experience, God the Spirit comes to know the most proper prayer for us in crying out "Abba" (Gal 4:6; Rom 8:26-7), the supreme Spirit-Christological prayer. The Holy Spirit has gained this particular human experience through accompanying the Son and Mary right from the annunciation to the cross. Once again, we note von Balthasar's constant hermeneutic — the horizon of the prayer of unity rooted in the mutual being for one another of the three divine Persons in the unity of the Godhead.

Mary's Magnificat and the Revolution of Love

Mary's yes at the annunciation is said in solitude, but it launches her into a journey which is communitarian. With the key word "behold, I am the servant of the Lord" to guide her,

33. Von Balthasar, "Maria und der Geist," 174; Tossou, *Streben nach Vollendung*, 363, fn. 3, and 337.
34. *Explorations III: Creator Spirit*, 123.
35. *Test Everything*, 43-47.

she enters a radically new phase of letting it be done "according to your word." She no longer makes her plans but lets herself be guided, in the words of Irenaeus, by the "two hands" of God, her Son, Jesus Christ and the Spirit. She is taken up into a new rhythm of life. And in this sense, the relationship of love between the divine Persons is constantly seen in her. She is inhabited by the Word and lives totally for the Word made flesh. And the Word, Jesus Christ, is totally directed toward the Father. Just as the Spirit lives in and upon Jesus, so too Mary follows the promptings of the Spirit.

God has taken the initiative in the annunciation, but the movement of the incarnation is directed toward everyone. It is a movement of "enfleshment" of the Word in our world and history, and the drawing of our world and history into the unity of God. In Mary, the Son is under way toward his "hour," the hour in which the Word is to become eucharist and Church for the whole of humanity. In Mary, humanity is already directed toward the Son. Mary's journey, therefore, is never an isolated one but rather directed toward and lived with others.

In the visitation scene, we see that Mary is aware of the dimensions of what has happened. She visits her cousin Elizabeth to make herself useful. But in the course of the visit the opportunity arises for the cousins to recognize each other's grace and share their joy. This is the moment for Mary to tell her experience of what God has done in her life, because she wants "to give her light to everyone in the house."[36] Her song, the Magnificat (Lk 1:46-55), tells of a "revolution of love" that has begun in her.[37] Love has poured itself down upon earth, and it is Mary's lowliness and humility that lies at the heart of this "divine revolution" beginning among us. Mary does not believe in herself but rather in God's deed "for the Almighty has done great things for me."

---

36. *You Have Words of Eternal Life,* 139.
37. *Mary for Today,* 59.

Mary understands more than any other that everything is a matter of grace. What is happening is not of her doing. But she also knows that the freedom granted her is in view of this "revolution" which is exploding in the world. Her Magnificat tells of its social and historical implications. There will be no line of demarcation between her unique experience and the countless generations to come. Because she has been drawn into the triune life of God in a unique fashion, Mary has entered into an inward communion of destiny with all generations which are to be brought within God's encompassing mercy and freedom. Von Balthasar comments that Mary is liberation theology in person.[38]

In the Presence of Jesus

Along with Thérèse of Lisieux, Bernanos, and Péguy, von Balthasar is fascinated by the mystery of Mary's pregnancy, Jesus' birth and childhood.[39] He recognizes the importance of the mother-child relationship that philosophy, sociology and psychology have brought to light in recent dialogue with one another. Today there is ever greater recognition of the active role of the mother in a child's conception, gestation and birth, as well as her importance in the early years of a child's education. Accordingly, von Balthasar reminds us that Mary's contribution to Jesus' conception, birth and upbringing is not to be underestimated.

He invites us firstly to contemplate the mysterious dialogue within the one substance during the nine months of pregnancy. Mary and her child are one flesh and their unity the model of any unity in the world. In his theology of history he comments that since the child-mother relationship is the most

38. *Mary for Today*, 59. See also von Balthasar's article, "Heilsgeschichtliche überlegungen zur Befreiungstheologie," in Karl Lehmann et al, *Theologie der Befreiung* (Einsiedeln: Johannes Verlag, 1977), 155-171.
39. For the following see *Man in History*, 249ff; *Prayer*, 201ff; "Maria in der kirchlichen Lehre," 45-48.

intimate and concrete meeting ever between divine history
and human history, it brings us to the deepest chamber of the
theology of history.[40] Both the past and future are caught up in
the eternity that she carries within her (Lk 1:55).

The mother-child relationship begins with a blind sense of
touch that will extend to the seeing and hearing which comes
with birth. But the time of pregnancy is also a time of anxiety
for Mary. Von Balthasar sees this anxiety during her pregnancy as a kind of "pre-passion" and in this too she embodies
the messianic "labor pains" of Israel's history.

The birth of the child Jesus brings joy. The Son's "repose in
the bosom of the Father, his being turned toward the Father"
(Jn 1:18) takes on the form of warmly being nestled in the
arms of his mother. But this birth also means a detachment for
Mary, something of the sword that is to pierce her soul.

Mary's role in Jesus' early formation is crucial to his
mission. He learns so much from his mother. From her lips the
child hears and repeats the human sound of the name of the
Father. Mary passes on the divine tradition of her people of
Israel. She gives wonderful example, not least in teaching Jesus
what it is to renounce. She introduces him to her own
renouncing which, as we have just seen, commences with his
birth.

Jesus is initiated into Mary's assent to God. His gratitude to
her is similar to that shown to the heavenly Father, who per-
mitted him to become man so as to bring the world back to
God. Such is Mary's freedom and engagement in the revolution of love that in her Jesus learns in human terms that the
human restrictions arising from original sin can really be over-
come and collapse. He can envision what a new humanity as-
senting to God is like.

Describing the life of the family of Nazareth, von Balthasar
imagines it as one bound by the prescriptions and rules of nor-
mal family life. In his obedience to his Father's will, Jesus is
obedient within the human community of this family, because

---

40. *Theologie der Geschichte*, 46.

this is his home. But there is something more. For Mary and Joseph it is a place of the attractive joy that flows from being in the presence of God who has assumed human form in Jesus. At its inner heart are the liberating evangelical counsels of poverty, chastity and obedience, the form of life that the presence of Jesus brings.[41] Such is the atmosphere of this family of Nazareth that it is also a school of mutual education. Just as the child is taught by his mother, Mary is taught by her Son. She grows in insight and begins to learn what her ultimate role will be. She sees Jesus grow in grace, not only in the sense of being full of the Holy Spirit, but also in terms of human goodness, affability and moral attractiveness. This is a period of joy and light for Mary. A thoroughly human as well as supernatural joy.

Living the Word and Being Alert to the Spirit

The "revolution of love" brought about by the Holy Spirit at the annunciation, and Mary's journey in the presence of the Word made flesh, do not remove her from everyday life but fill every event with new life. She journeys with her Son toward his "hour," and in this she is guided by God's "two hands," the Word and the Spirit. The numerous biblical references in the Magnificat tell us how much Mary lives from the biblical tradition. Mary's astute generosity at the wedding in Cana manifests just how alert she is to the Spirit where, von Balthasar notes, Mary, the woman, "disturbs" masculine planning.[42]

Among the early incidents in Mary's life that shaped her alertness to God's plan is the day of the presentation of the child Jesus in the Temple. It is of pivotal importance because it is the day when Simeon provides her with a road sign, indicating the direction of her life. It is true that, in the very act of

---

41. *Christian State of Life*, 207-208.
42. *The Grain of Wheat* (San Francisco: Ignatius Press, 1995), 66-67; *Office of Peter*, 208. Cf. Michel T'Joen, "Marie et l'ésprit," 167.

being born, there already began for Jesus, as for every human being, the act of dying. But Simeon, the inclusive representative of Israel, tells Mary how she will experience the universalization of the Covenant, the Jewish Law, in its expansion through the death of Jesus Christ. And this will mean the sword and the cross.

It is against this horizon that every day Mary begins to search for her way in obedience to God. Her life is to follow the "law" of life that Jesus outlined — if you lose your life you will find it (Lk 9:24). Losing and finding are to be the characteristics of her journey, signified early on by the episode of the losing and finding of the child Jesus in the Temple. But all of Mary's caring for her Son and her discipleship, her keeping and pondering all his words in her heart, will enable her to "penetrate more and more deeply into an understanding of the Trinity: of the Father whose daughter she is, of the Son whose mother and spiritual bride she is, and of the Spirit whose vessel she is."[43]

Forsaken with the Forsaken One

In von Balthasar's writings, Mary is *the* model of discipleship, a discipleship of transparency to Christ, because in the *sequela Christi* Mary lives outside herself. The light that Jesus brings is so new, so unique, that we can only be initiated into it by Jesus, by that experience which we have of him. He himself is the way we must tread if we want to understand the truth and the life. In living and following this "way," Mary too had to be initiated into what she was unable to understand (Lk 2:50).

Von Balthasar notices the various moments Jesus seems to rebuff Mary in the gospel (such as at the finding of the child in the Temple, at Cana, at two moments of rejection during his

---

43. *Prayer*, 195.

public ministry and at the cross). These negative moments, however, serve a purpose. Mary is the one woman who truly belongs to the new covenant. The rejections she experiences are a mode of illustrating what Jesus' disciples have to transcend in order to enter into the novelty of the family (Mt 12:46-50) that the Son of God came on earth to establish: "Flesh and blood cannot inherit the kingdom of God" (1 Cor 15:50). Physical descent alone is not an entrance ticket into the new family of Jesus. Rather, doing the will of God is. And this can be seen in what von Balthasar considers as perhaps Mary's most beautiful saying: "Do whatever he tells you" (Jn 2:5).[44]

Mary's yes is so pure, unlimited and definitive that it includes all the destiny of the Son whom she affirms at the annunciation. And since the destiny of the Son of God who took on our sinful human nature is the cross ("whoever says incarnation thereby says the cross"[45]), Mary's destiny is always beneath the shadow of the cross:[46]

> The sword that was to pierce Mary so that "the thoughts of many hearts should be revealed" (Lk 2:35) did not cease piercing her; it has kept the whole insistence of her consent awake for this day, on which its terrible depths would be plumbed. Mary's consent, her spiritual and physical readiness, is responsible for the earthly existence of Jesus, who perfects the Old Covenant and brings the promise of the New and Eternal Covenant; it prefigures the coming Church of Jesus; and it has a decisive role to play on the cross. It is to mediate between God's faithless covenant partners, who have adopted Gentile ways ("we have no king but Caesar," Jn 19:15), and the future covenant-partners

---

44. "Our Lady in Monasticism," 52-56, here 55.
45. See von Balthasar's famous article on the paschal mystery published in book form as *Threefold Garland Paschale*, espec. 12ff; *Glory of the Lord* VII, 202ff.
46. *Theo-Drama IV*, 353ff. In *Explorations III: Creator Spirit*, 224ff, von Balthasar refers us to Adrienne von Speyr's description of the feminine dimension at the cross in terms of the "mystery of the three Marys": Mary of Bethany, Mary of Magdala and Mary, the mother of Jesus.

who will come to faith through the grace of the "Lamb as though it had been slain." It is not easy to situate this role in the whole drama.[47]

When Jesus' hour arrives, a second major yes is required of Mary.[48] In this dark period, the Holy Spirit continues to overshadow Mary but this time, von Balthasar comments, with what was most fruitful: the dark night of the senses and of the spirit. Both Jesus and Mary, the softest of hearts, must be tempered for representation's sake. And at the passion we see this representation in all its starkness.

The passion is Jesus' decisive deed: He admits sin's monstrous darkness into himself. This is his hour. Jesus' death on the cross is presented by von Balthasar as an icon of the eternal dialogue of love happening in God. The cross involves the mutual surrender out of love of the Father and Son in the unity of the Holy Spirit.

In God's plan, Mary's role is set into this event in a vital, albeit paradoxical, fashion. She vanishes anonymously into the crowd, so much so that the synoptic gospels do not even notice her among the women at the foot of the cross. Echoing Jesus' solidarity with sinners, and his taking on of their sin, Mary's immaculate solidarity means that she is placed at the "last place," behind the last of the sinners.

Manifesting both the depths of God's love for the world and the truth of its sin, the Son takes on all the darkness of the sin of the world and continues loving right to the point of abandonment on the cross. Now as he is returning to the Father, Jesus' mission from the Father takes on the paradoxical form of going away from the Father toward the world.[49] His cry of forsakenness on the cross, the highest point of the history of revelation, is a cry that embraces all humankind's nostalgia for God, all our questions searching for an answer.[50]

---

47. *Theo-Drama IV*, 353.
48. Cf. Adrienne von Speyr, *Handmaid of the Lord*, 113-121.
49. See Rudolf Krenski, *Passio Caritatis: Trinitarische Passiologie im Werk Hans Urs von Balthasar* (Einsiedeln: Johannes Verlag, 1990).
50. *Theo-Drama I*, 21.

Mary's yes is to be repeated in the midst of all of this. While she has disappeared into the crowds, her yes doesn't simply disappear into Jesus' yes at the cross. Her renewed yes has vital significance in the drama. She is the "helper" and "bride" who suffers with her Son to the degree assigned to her. She is to echo his forsakenness. In this, Abraham's faith is to reach the extreme consequence in Mary, because no angel intervenes, and she has to give the Father back his Son, the Son of the fulfillment.

Mary both facilitates and embodies the goal of the event of the cross. This is her paradoxical role in the drama of redemption. Inundated in a light radiating from the crucified Christ and standing before him, Mary is the Father's indication to the Son, in an incarnational and inner-historical manner, of the newly redeemed humanity and creation. But this remains objectively unrecognizable to him. Mary is no longer a sign for Christ of his origins or of the future. If anything, given her purity, she seems to indicate how superfluous his mission has been. And she is also now to appear as most distant from him:

> Hidden behind the multitude of sinners, embracing them all, she is objectively closest to him: she makes his suffering possible and guarantees its goal. Now, however, he can only see her as the farthest from him; this is how he *must* see her. He is forsaken absolutely, and the only way of communion with him is to take leave of him and plunge into forsakenness. He must withdraw from his Mother just as the Father has withdrawn from him: "Woman, behold your son."[51]

Just as the Father is hidden from the Son, now Mary experiences abandonment by the Son, as she stands behind all the division of the world's sin. Mary's poverty of spirit reaches the point of being detached from everything, even from the maternity of her Son. There could be no greater test than this — to

---

51. *Theo-Drama IV*, 356.

consent to the total abandonment of her Son and by her Son. At this point, Mary's is a superhuman action.

She, the Seat of Wisdom, sees in the torn body and, particularly, the spiritual anguish of her Son's Godforsakenness, the whole truth about the fallen world. She communes with the sufferings of her Son and experiences in her own manner just what the sin of the world really is like.

Paradoxically, now both the forsaken Son and the forsaken Mother are united in a mutual forsakenness. Von Balthasar remarks how there is nothing more incomprehensible and supernatural in Mary's life than the fact that she does not die with the Son because she lives by the Son no less than he lives by the Father. While not understanding, Mary allows herself to be used for his goals, which are hidden in the darkest night. Hers is a spiritual death, a non-bloody martyrdom.

Mary and John the Evangelist

The Fourth Gospel depicts Mary and John the Evangelist present together at the cross.[52] The evangelist describes Jesus' last act on earth: "When Jesus saw his mother, and the disciple whom he loved standing near, he said to his mother, 'Woman, behold your son!' Then he said to the disciple, 'Behold, your mother!' And from that hour the disciple took her to his own home" (Jn 19:27). Henceforth John is to live with Mary as a son.

We know that the evangelist is communicating theological depths in this passage. Jesus is generating a "new family" on the cross. And in doing so he transfers Mary's motherhood to a new son, John, the beloved disciple, who represents Peter, the whole group of the Twelve and ultimately all of us, as the last chapter of John's gospel shows us. This new union between Mary and John is the last thing that Jesus established by

---

52. See *Glory of the Lord* VII, 196ff; *Mary for Today*, 52-55. Cf. Adrienne von Speyr, *Handmaid of the Lord*, 122-131.

indicating a new way of living, one that comes about through and beyond the cross. Citing Ephraem, von Balthasar points to the novelty of their relationship: they reciprocally see Christ in one another.[53] It is a new covenant, the covenant of God among us.

At this point, Mary has reached her final and irreversible state of life and, from now on, her life with John will be lived on the supernatural level. A new life of communion has been born. John and the whole community of believers begin to fill the place prepared for them. Mary has become their mother. Now the world has become Jesus' place and is to be loved for his sake. Now God is to be found in our brothers and sisters, in the world, in the "least."

But what of Holy Saturday, the "non-time" of silence? Does the mystery of Christ's descent among the dead involve Mary? Von Balthasar refers to the poetry of Romanos the Melode who, in hymn 35, sings of Mary at the foot of the cross in dialogue with her Son. Jesus explains to her how, like a doctor, he is going to have to strip himself of his clothes in order to reach the place where the mortally ill are lying and heal them. Mary pleads to be taken with him, but he warns her that the whole creation will be shaken, earth and sea will flee away, the mountains will tremble and the tombs will be emptied.

At this point the dialogue breaks off. On the one hand, echoing Adrienne von Speyr, von Balthasar contends that participation in Christ's descent into the hell of the dead could not be included in Mary's initial yes,[54] and yet, he also states that the loving Church (represented by the three Marys) is expected to accompany him there.[55] What we do know is that from Good Friday to Easter Sunday Mary is deprived of the

---

53. *Mary for Today* 50. Cf. Mar Aprem, *H Virg* 25:9 (Jn 19:26-27) in Pierre Yousif, "Marie et le disciple bien-aimé," 302-303.
54. *Threefold Garland Paschale*, 50-51. See Von Speyr, *Die Nachlasswerke: IV: Kreuz und Hölle* (Einsiedeln: Johannes Verlag, 1966), 49, 80, 120ff, 134, 141, 144, 147ff, 316-324.
55. *Die Wahrheit ist symphonisch: Aspekte des christlichen Pluralismus* (Einsiedeln: Johannes Verlag, 1972), 144; Adrienne von Speyr, *Die Nachlasswerke I/2: Allerheiligenbuch* (Einsiedeln: Johannes Verlag, 1977), 205.

center of her soul, her Son. It is the Father and the Holy Spirit who keep her supernaturally erect.[56]

---

56. *Christian State of Life,* 208-209.

Mary, Woman Whose Mission Continues between Time and Eternity

The death of Jesus is not the end of the Christian story. "If Christ has not been raised, then our faith is in vain" (1 Cor 15:14). Death is only one side of the trinitarian icon presented in the paschal mystery. Jesus' resurrection is the Father's seal of approval on the Son's mission. In the resurrection the purpose of Jesus' death is made manifest: to make us children of the Father in the freedom of the Spirit. Accordingly, the resurrection marks the beginning of the new Christian movement, which is to spread throughout the world.

Regarding the origins of Christianity, the New Testament tells us that Mary is to be found in the midst of the Christian community praying (Acts 1:14). She is the woman of the third day, and her mission continues as she accompanies the people of the eighth day, the new creation. Rooted in the eternal dialogue between the Father and the Son, her mission is continued by the Spirit as one that spans time and eternity. The Book of Revelation points out to us this definitive state of Mary as the woman "in between" heaven and earth (Rv 12), the woman whose mission continues between time and eternity.

Pentecost

While scripture does not explicitly state anything about Mary and the resurrection, von Balthasar follows some of the Fathers of the Church, Ignatius of Loyola and Hopkins, believing the risen Lord appeared firstly to Mary at the very core of the Church.[57] Neither does scripture tell us whether Mary was present at the ascension. Von Balthasar comments that the period after the ascension is another renunciation for Mary: She loses her Son definitively placing him in the hands of the Father.[58] Where we do see Mary is at prayer with the early Christian community. The Holy Spirit had first descended upon her, and now she prays in the midst of the community that what occurred in her may occur again. And this is fulfilled at Pentecost.

Regarding Pentecost von Balthasar refers us to Guardini, who comments that there must have been something divinely great when, by the light of the Spirit, everything became clear to Mary "who had kept all these things in her heart (Lk 2:51)."[59] It was a clarifying light that solved everything. From her initial yes at the annunciation, the Holy Spirit had breathed through Mary's whole being and initiated her into the truth of the mutual love of the Father and the Son which he is. Now this Spirit descends upon her anew endowing her with new light and life.

Before Pentecost, Mary was protected from understanding the full import of two statements concerning Jesus: "He is the Son of the eternal Father" and "He is your Son." At Pentecost the new light from heaven enables her to bear this understanding without breaking down or becoming confused. At Pentecost the Spirit presents to her the content of her own experience as her memory had retained it:

> What is unique about her is that the Spirit of Pentecost basically does nothing other than to present to her the content of her own experience as her memory had retained it, a memory that contains all the central dogmas of revelation in their complete unity and interwovenness.[60]

---

57. *Threefold Garland*, 112. Cf. Ignatius of Loyola, *Spiritual Exercises*, n. 299.
58. *Threefold Garland*, 118.
59. *Mary for Today*, 37-41.
60. *Mary for Today*, 39.

In following Jesus during her life, Mary was led higher and higher in the way of discipleship. At Pentecost, she recognizes the ineffable content of her vocation and mission. The risen Christ leads her into the Church of Pentecost.[61]

Assumption [62]

What can we say about the end of Mary's earthly life? Von Balthasar writes that death was God's final will for Mary to which she submitted willingly. It was the final form of her letting it happen according to the primary word that guided her in life: "Be it done to me according to your word." All of us advance toward a final state of union with God in heaven. Death is our ultimate initiation into the limitless depth and breadth of the loving God's threefold gift of self.

As for the nature of Mary's death, because it is so closely associated with her assumption into heaven, von Balthasar simply asks: "Who could attempt to express it in the categories available to us?" Mary is mortal, she is not a goddess; there may have been nothing extraordinary about the death of the "lowly handmaid." The earliest Church documents speak of her "death," but attempts to describe it flounder. Dormition is a word to express the unique experience of death of this woman who, in the words of John Damascene "made death bright and banished its sadness" because, having already shared in her Son's death, she proclaimed joy in her death.

The joy proclaimed is that of the assumption. Legends of Mary's death and subsequent elevation to heaven date back possibly as early as the second century. But, in von Balthasar's opinion, legendary elements were quickly replaced by solid reasoning arising out of a consideration of Mary's central place in the history of salvation. He refers to a homily on the assumption by Theodosius of Alexandria (566) in which the

---

61. "Our Lady in Monasticism," 53.
62. See *Threefold Garland,* 127ff; *Theo-Drama III,* 336ff; *Mary for Today,* 29ff.

following words are attributed to Jesus in presenting his
mother to the heavenly Father: "Accept her who received your
only Son in the world; your holy Temple, who was the dwelling place of your Holy Spirit." Theodosius proceeds to tell how
Mary is delivered from death and transfigured in the presence
of God. Now she is given a share in her Son's working of freeing us from death: "Now that you are free, stand up and bear to
the ends of the earth this freedom with which I have ransomed
my entire creation."[63]

Mary, whose life echoed Christ's, totally shares in his glori-
fication. She who gave herself completely and unconditionally
to God the Father, has reached heaven — that fullness of life,
joy and perfection promised to those who hand themselves
over to God. It was centuries of reflection upon scripture texts
and consideration of Mary's life, as well as deeper perception
of how her soul and body were so indivisibly united at God's
disposal, that led the Church to define Mary's assumption. In
the same wholeness with which she gave of herself to God she
has been taken up to where she has always had her "place."[64]
She has gone "home" to paradise, the place she recognizes as
the one in which she has always been. The immaculate word of
assent that she uttered at the annunciation and repeated right
through life has drawn her back into heaven in her totality.[65]

The Apocalyptic Image

The Book of Revelation presents the image of a woman crying in the wilderness (Rv 12). Von Balthasar interprets this in
a Marian-ecclesial framework. In fact, this is a central image in
von Balthasar's Mariology, one which leads us into the next
chapter on the continuing mission of Mary in the Church, so
that at this point we need only mention some aspects.[66]

---

63. *Theo-Drama III*, 336. Cf. M. Chaine in *Rev. de l'orient chrétien* 29 (1933-1934), 272-314.
64. *Mary for Today*, 30. See also *You Crown the Year*, 186-200.
65. *Threefold Garland*, 128.
66. See *Mary for Today*, 7ff. Cf. I. de la Potterie, *Mary in the Mystery of the Covenant*, 243ff.

Firstly, the cosmic vision of this twelfth chapter of the Apocalypse presents the "in-between" situation of Mary's continuing mission. In von Balthasar's opinion, it is unthinkable that a Christian writer at the end of the first century, using the image of Zion in labor and giving birth to the person of the Messiah, should not have had in mind the physical mother of Jesus, particularly if she was close to the compiler of the Fourth Gospel.[67] Mary's further destiny is located between heaven and earth.

While on earth, Mary lived the "eschatological tension" of bearing the mark of paradise but walking in the pains of birth and life's difficulties. The Apocalyptic writer tells us that she has "fled into the desert" where she has a place prepared for her by God, but the dragon, in his great wrath, opposes her. Her crying in travail is symbolic of her life lived now in the "in-between." Having taken her place in paradise, she is intimately involved in the formation of a new humanity. She continues to give birth, and that to which she gives birth is fruit for eternal life:

> The tension must emerge if Mary is the true Mother of all the living, who, though she has regained paradise (in her Immaculate Conception), gives birth to the Messiah-scion and his brothers and sisters in the birth-pangs of the cross, as is appropriate within the confines of fallen nature. Or, we could say, as is inevitable, given the vulnerability of an innocent being in the midst of fallenness (cf. Isaiah 26:17 and 66:7-9 taken together, in connection with Revelation 12). That to which Mary gives birth, out of the virginal purity of paradise yet in the pains of time and the "desert" (Rv 12:6), is fruit for eternal life.[68]

In giving birth from paradise, Mary's theodramatic role continues in this world. On earth, writes von Balthasar, Mary

---

67. *Theo-Drama III*, 334-335. See also Ugo Vanni, *Apocalisse: Esegesi dei brani scelti* (Rome: PIB, 1992-93), n.V.
68. *Theo-Drama III*, 334.

was the contemplative par excellence, in heaven she has become the most active of all.[69]

Conclusion

This part has looked at some features of Mary's role in the drama of redemption. In von Balthasar's writings, she is very clearly the supreme "work of God," and everything about her speaks of the triune life that first opened before our eyes at the annunciation. Excogitated in the mystery of God's free and loving decision to create, save and, as the Eastern tradition puts it, "divinize" us, Mary echoes features of the unity of God's own triune life. She is the woman, writes von Balthasar, "in whom the triune life is fulfilled."[70]

Within God, the *Father* is the unoriginated source and origin of love. On earth, Mary, formed in God's eternal mystery, is the earthly source of love, protection, and nurturing for the Son. Her love made room for the new life of the incarnate Son. As virgin and "servant of the Lord" she is an unlimited openness in love.

Within God, *the Son* is receptive vis-à-vis the Father. Mary echoes in a creaturely fashion the inner receptivity of the Son. Mary is able to welcome love, to receive love. Her poverty and humility consist in that lack of possessiveness which allows the incarnation to happen. She lets herself be loved. As well as offering herself as "home" for the Son of God, her "poverty" of receiving is the condition of possibility for communion with God. Mary's yes is pure and total response to God's initiative in the incarnation and paschal mystery. It is a response that grows from perfection to perfection until its culmination at the cross.

Within God, *the Spirit* is the bond of unity between the Father and the Son and the opening of that divine communion

---

69. "Our Lady in Monasticism," 55.
70. *Prayer*, 195.

toward us. Mary is Woman "overshadowed" by the Holy Spirit to become the mother of God. Hers is not a closed "I – God" relationship. Her mission is inclusive of others, indeed, of all others. Totally rooted in God, she is in perfect solidarity with our human condition. She lives totally for *the* "Other" (God), and she lives and embraces each "other" (the human race) by representing them.

Mary is a woman of mission because she is so deeply a woman of communion. She is a woman of communion because her "home" is the unity of the divine mystery of God, who wants to be "all in all." In Mary we see the pouring out of the divine dialogue of love upon humanity, and humanity's being raised up to share in the eternal "event" of unity that sets us free.

Part 4

The Marian Principle in the Church

In the introduction to *Spouse of the Word,* von Balthasar invites us to view the Church as "a mystery of love, to be approached only with reverence."[1] He wants us to glance through the many windows which open unto her mystery and glimpse at aspects often previously unsuspected. Having in the previous chapters prepared the way, the following pages aim to be one such window. We want to look at the mystery of the Church through the window of her Marian principle. To let von Balthasar guide us more directly in this meditation, we'll cite his texts more abundantly.

When he writes on this theme, there are three biblical icons that are important for him. The first is what might be called an icon of *mystery.* It comes from Paul's letter to the Ephesians, a letter that is central in von Balthasar's ecclesiology.[2] In its opening hymn (Eph 1:1-10) Paul paints with broad brush strokes the lavish nature of God's mystery unfolding in his eternal trinitarian plan "to unite all things in Christ." It is depicted as a torrent of grace. And in chapter 5 of the same letter, Paul leads us to marvel at the "great mystery," Christ and the Church.

The second biblical icon has *communion* as its theme. This time John the Evangelist is the artist. The subject matter is Jesus' "farewell discourse" leading into and including the

---

1. *Explorations II: Spouse of the Word,* 7.
2. He is guided in his exegetical interpretation of the Letter to the Ephesians by Heinrich Schlier, *Der Brief an die Epheser* (Einsiedeln, 1957) and Adrienne von Speyr, *Kinder des Lichtes: Betrachtungen über den Epheserbrief* (Vienna: Verlag Herold, 1949). See also von Balthasar, *Mein Werk: Durchblicke* (Einsiedeln: Johannes Verlag, 1990), 86.

scene of Jesus' death (Jn 14-19). John depicts Christ journeying from and back to the Trinity. It is a journey which brings us
"home" within the bosom of the Father.[3] The Church, represented at the foot of the cross by Mary and John, is depicted as
a community of faith and love. She is to act as the mediation
between the love-unity in the triune God and the love-unity of
all humanity created to share in this life in Christ.

Mission is the motif of the third icon. It is based on
chapter 12 of the Book of Revelation seen through a Marian
lens.[4] It is the vision of the woman crying out in travail.
Linking it with Mary's giving birth to Jesus, and her role in the
birth of the mystical body at the foot of the cross, von
Balthasar's reading of this icon is that Mary has been "expropriated" and given to the whole Church in her mission upon
earth. Throughout history, this woman-Mary-Church cries
out in travail giving birth to Christ. Mary is linked to the mission of the Church, as we already participate in and head
toward the eschatological scene depicted in Revelation 21-22.

It is on the basis of these and other such biblical icons that von
Balthasar meditates on the Marian principle in the Church. As we
have seen, together with Adrienne von Speyr he uses the couplet
"Mary-Church" to express his view that there is a mutual indwelling of Mary and the Church. Certainly, the sphere of the Church
is Christ's and he is her consciousness. But since the countenance
of the whole Church is a responsive one, von Balthasar writes of
Mary's archetypal experience of faith, her yes, as having flown
into the life of the Church as her highest normative subjectivity,
personal center, and fundamental *realsymbol.*[5] He also writes of a
specific Marian principle operative within the life-sphere of the

---

3. See *Theologik III*, 399ff. See Hans O. Meuffels, *Einbergung des Menschen in das Mysterium der dreieinigen Liebe: eine trinitarische Anthropologie nach Hans Urs von Balthasar* (Würzburg: Echter Verlag, 1991).

4. See *Mary for Today*, 7ff; *You Crown the Year*, 188; *Theo-Drama III*, 335ff. We are referred to A. Feuillet, "Le Messie et sa mère, d'après le chap XII de l'Apocalypse," *Revue Biblique* 66 (1959), espec. 80; F. M. Braun, *La Mère des Fidèles: Essai de Théologie Johannique* (Paris: Casterman, 1954), 147-153; L. Cerfaux, "La vision de la femme et du dragon etc," *Eph. theol. Lov* (1955), 21-33; Newman, *Difficulties of Anglicans* (New York, 1930), 3:58-59.

5. *Office of Peter*, 204, 224-225; *Explorations II: Spouse of the Word*, 179; *Explorations III: Creator Spirit*, 295-296.

Church. God has given us Mary as an all-embracing principle, a meeting point, as it were, between the various dimensions of the Church.[6]

The reflection that follows here shall be guided by the framework which we have just expressed above in iconic form — mystery-communion-mission. In terms of the Church's origins in the *mystery* of the triune God, we shall look at the Marian openness and availability (the "servant of the Lord," *Ancilla Domini*) at the heart of the Church. The link between the Marian principle and the life of *communion* in the Church will then be examined from the perspective of the Church as bride of the Word (*Sponsa Verbi*). The third dimension to be examined shall be the Marian principle from the perspective of the Church's *mission* (*Mater Dei et Mater Ecclesiae*).

---

6. *Office of Peter,* 183-225, 308ff. Cf. Adrienne von Speyr, *Handmaid of the Lord,* 148-153.

The Church's Marian Principle and Mystery
(Servant of the Lord)

To say that the Church is a "miracle of love" is von Balthasar's way of underlining a central thesis that no matter how much the Church may present herself as an object of inquiry to the historian, the religious or profane sociologist or to many other specialists, her origins are to be found in the mystery of God, and her form is relative to Jesus Christ from whom she has emerged.[7] We are born in the *mystery* of the triune God of love revealed to us in Jesus Christ. It is in his death and resurrection that the Church has been generated. As the "servant of the Lord" (Lk 1:38) (*Ancilla Domini*), Mary has been given to us as a model precisely so that we might never forget our homeland in God.

Emphasis on the mystery also explains why, in considering the Church's origins, von Balthasar holds that one has to leave calculation of exact moments aside. Because of their unique nature, the various moments such as the annunciation, the crucifixion and Pentecost are only to be called historical events in an analogous manner. They are events which have neither historical end nor historical beginning in the full sense of the word. Rather, they are the "historical" making present of a supra-temporal eternal reality within history.[8]

Various passages of scripture (Gal 4:26; Rv 21:2; Eph 5) speak of the Church as a heavenly reality, hidden and dwelling with God (Heb 12:22).[9] Many patristic writers such as Clement, Shepherd of Hermas, Origen, Augustine and Methodius of Olympia wrote of the original spiritual Church founded, as

---

7. See *Office of Peter,* 287-307; *Glory of the Lord I,* 556-604.
8. *Man in History,* 114.
9. See also Heb 1:3ff; 2 Tm 1:9; 1 Pt 1:20; Eph 5. See H. Schlier, *Der Brief an die Galater* (Göttingen: Vandenhoeck & Ruprecht, 1955), 221-226; L. Cerfaux, *La Théologie de l'église suivant Saint Paul* (Paris: Cerf, 1965), 305-312.

Clement puts it, "before the moon and the sun." Von Balthasar is attracted by the basic insight in their writings, namely, that the deepest origins of the Church are to be traced right back through the broad sweep of creation and salvation history into the very source of love: God.

In the light of the Church Fathers' writings, von Balthasar too writes of a holy, supra-temporal Church.[10] He understands the Church's supra-temporality, however, not so much in terms of an existence before the world began but rather in terms of a supra-historical and eschatological reality that has to do with us here and now. The supra-temporal dimension of the Church is what he calls the "heavenly Church" that accompanies us.

This notion of a supra-temporal or heavenly Church is not to be understood, therefore, in a dualistic or gnostic sense. We don't have two separate Churches, one which is pure and heavenly, and the other which is sinful, earthly and on pilgrimage upon this earth. The earthly and the heavenly Church are one reality in Christ. By his emphasis on the heavenly Church, von Balthasar wants to remind us that there is a spiritual pulley at the heart of the ecclesial sphere. And it is in this context that he underlines the ecclesiological significance of Mary's immaculate conception.

The liturgy applies the following wisdom text to Mary: "Ages ago I was set up, at the first, before the beginning of the earth" (Prv 8:23), and in so doing wants to link God's unique plan for Mary with our election in Christ. We have been chosen "in him [Christ] before the foundation of the world" to become members of his body-bride. Christ gave his life so "that he might sanctify her [his bride the Church], having cleansed her by the washing of water with the word, that he might present the Church to himself in splendor, without spot or wrinkle or any such thing, that she might be holy and without blemish" (Eph 1:4; 5:25-27). Mary's immaculate conception is God's gift to us of the perfect yes that embraces all of us

---

10. *Explorations IV: Spirit and Institution*, 125-138; *Homo Creatus Est*, 148ff.

and shapes our election as children of God being formed into the bridal-body of Christ. As some Eastern texts tell us, Mary is a human "second heaven" who received the "heaven" of the Son of God come among us.[11]

The ecclesiological significance of Mary's immaculate conception is linked by von Balthasar with a broad horizon of Church identity. Because of Mary's immaculate yes there is a universal heavenly dimension of the Church that accompanies us here and now in the midst of temporality:

> The heavenly Church is certainly not God, but it is in God and draws life totally from him. On earth she has the task of protecting and administering the living work of Christ throughout time as a work that is constantly present . . . nevertheless she is capable of doing this only because her work center and the center from which her work irradiates are in Christ. Never separated from the heavenly Church, he works his salvation on earth through the earthly forms and institutions of the Church. . . . Mary is not only one link among others in the heavenly Church, but for many reasons she is the essence of this Church of heaven.[12]

Von Balthasar writes of the Christ-Mary union as the fundamental "cell" of the Church. He goes on then to say that, speaking improperly and analogously, the Church participates in Christ's kenosis by letting herself be led in whatever direction God chooses.[13] In her inner core, she is formed by the inspirations from "above," from the Holy Spirit, and not by her own will. The fundamental attitude that echoes in her inner depths is that of the "handmaid of the Lord" (*Ancilla Domini*), who allows the gift of the trinitarian life of love to shape her in Christ:

---

11. See "Common Prayer for the Feasts of Our Lady" in *Khodra*, vol.1 (Trichur, India: Mar Narsai Press, 1962), 609, 593.
12. *Homo Creatus Est*, 149ff.
13. See *Explorations IV: Spirit and Institution*, 125ff.

Insofar as this sphere [the Church] is his own, he [Christ] is her consciousness; and insofar as she makes to him the response of a woman and a bride, she has her supreme, normative subjectivity in Mary. Finally, insofar as the one grace streams through her, this grace makes all spirits, in all their personal varieties of missions and spiritual ways, converge in a single consciousness, opening in Mary to Christ, and through Christ to the Holy Spirit of the three-personal God, who in the beginning overshadowed Mary and, since Easter and Pentecost, dwells in the Church.[14]

On the basis of his considerations, von Balthasar draws a number of conclusions. Firstly, he makes a link with the Old Testament. In view of the universal dimensions of Mary's immaculate yes, von Balthasar points to a re-reading of the Old Testament history. It clearly manifests the upward movement of earth toward God. It is a covenant-history that unfolds, making room for communion with God. But the whole Old Testament community of salvation is inwardly linked and culminates in a certain sense in Mary. In her, Israel passes into the Church. True to the Old Testament history, however, the doctrine of the Immaculate Conception tells us that all building up of communion is at God's initiative. The whole Old Testament history itself is enveloped in some way by this gift of the Immaculate Conception.

There is another element that von Balthasar wants to highlight, namely, the implications arising from the Marian dynamic of love at the heart of the Church for the issue of sinfulness in the Church. As a result of a certain contraction brought about by the doctrine of predestination taught by Augustine in his later years, a dualism crept into our understanding of Church membership. A mindset of barriers between Church and non-Church emerged. It is von Balthasar's contention that an appreciation of the ecclesiological significance of the Immaculate Conception of

---

14. *Explorations II: Spouse of the Word*, 179-180.

Mary is linked to a razing of false dualisms and a renewed appreciation of the universal dimensions of the Church's communion and outreach:

> The image of the Church, that of dynamic love bearing and being borne . . . an image that sees in the Church all gradations of holiness from the highest, most unsullied sanctity of Mary to the very brink of damnation, in fact even beyond it, in the case of the gravely sinful who are yet, in some way, members of the Church — this image is the justification of these two statements: that the Church, the more "properly" she is the Church, the more immaculate, the more conformed to Christ she is, the more Marian, and that she still remains the Church even in the sinner since the sinner has some velleity and is being borne by the suffering members of the Church, deficient and estranged though she herself may be, and as struggling and in course of conversion. The Church, at her core, remains immaculate and a pure bride. In this, she is distinguished from the synagogue, which according to the prophets, can become a brazen harlot.[15]

Having made these introductory points, let us now look at what von Balthasar considers to be the three foundational moments of the Church. In each case he sees Mary as the "source" into which the divine initiative could pour love. And he sees this as continuing in the heart of the Church. He calls the Marian-ecclesial openness to God a "space-affording medium" within which every sacramental grace can bear fruit and every charismatic service can develop as a service of love in keeping with the Church's open and catholic mission.[16]

---

15. *Explorations II: Spouse of the Word,* 179; Cf. Von Balthasar's article on this subject, "Casta Meretrix," in *Explorations II: Spouse of the Word,* 193-288.
16. See *New Elucidations,* 240.

The House of Nazareth

The house at Nazareth, writes von Balthasar, is where Christ's Church is "qualitatively" grounded, since at the incarnation Mary's yes provides the starting point for the New Testament and ecclesial faith. The annunciation is the encounter between God's "all" (of communion) and our readiness or openness to God. The result is that "atmosphere"[17] brought about both by the Holy Spirit and Mary's yes:

> The dialogue between the angel and Mary seems to be a purely private one, carried on in the "chamber" referred to in the Sermon on the Mount. But in this dialogue, as in every perfect prayer, two dimensions open up: God's all-in-all and humanity's complete readiness. And the Holy Spirit descends from the first to the second, bearing God's seed, the seed of the Word, to implant it in the earthly womb.[18]

Mary's yes is no mere individual response. There is a collective dimension of openness here. The communitarian "we" of the Church, formed by the divine "we," already finds expression in Mary's yes to God on behalf of the whole human race:[19]

> From the beginning, however, this Spirit is the divine "We": he is Person and community. When Mary is greeted, right from the outset, as "full of grace," this Spirit is already in her, fashioning the yes in her soul. Thus, whether she is aware of it or not, the community, the *Catholica* is already present in her yes; the whole faith of her people is ultimately formulated in it.[20]

---

17. Cf. *In the Fullness of Faith* 64; *Explorations IV: Spirit and Institution* 156.
18. *In the Fullness of Faith* 82-83.
19. *Explorations II: Spouse of the Word,* 163; *Theo-Drama IV,* 351-361. Cf. St. Thomas' dictum *"consensus virginis loco totius humanae naturae"* (*S. Th.* III, q. 30, a 1, c) and the other Aquinate dictum concerning Mary's consent radiating (*redundans*) on all of human nature (*S. Th.* 3 d 3, q 2 sol 2).
20. *In the Fullness of Faith,* 83.

In other words, Mary's yes is endowed by the Holy Spirit with a universality that recapitulates and embodies all moments of dedication and availability to God for all time:

> Indeed, it recapitulates whatever moment of dedication and readiness anyone ever had: according to Thomas Aquinas, Mary responds "on behalf of the entire human race." Therefore her yes is open to the future as well, sustaining all the attempts to say yes that will be made in the coming Church. The Church is already there, in perfection, in her, because the Spirit in whom she says yes is always God's "We," who has begun on earth his work of enabling us both to say "We" and to be "We."[21]

The virgin/mother-child union of the annunciation is a unique enfleshment of the "first cell" of the Church. It is a culminating moment in the whole divine project of salvation. The One whose constant operation is necessary for this project, the Holy Spirit, is very active just "as the Spirit will always be in the prayers and sacraments and charisms of the Church."[22]

The Cross

Von Balthasar sees the cross as *the* origin of the Church. Mary's totally inclusive love reaches the point at the foot of the cross where the entire people of God, *simul peccatores et justi,* is gathered for a second yes, a second conception. From the cross, Jesus places Mary firmly in the middle of his body, the Church, as the transparent openness receiving his eucharistically exuding body and his Spirit. Her openness to God is seen at the cross as a "letting be":

> Mary allows the cross to take place: this is the archetype of the Church's entire faith, which "allows things

---

21. *In the Fullness of Faith,* 83.
22. "Empfangen durch den Heiligen Geist," 47.

to take place" ("letting be"). This is seen particularly in the event of the eucharist, that existentially perfect and exemplary gesture that is implanted into the Church and handed down the centuries.[23]

Mary's second yes uttered at this culminating point of Jesus' self-giving, is not one historically single and past event. It is present throughout the history of the Church and mediated through Jesus Christ' perpetual making present of himself:

> Because he perpetually delivers himself anew, he is also perpetually delivered anew by his mother. Because he is constantly being conceived by believing albeit imperfect souls, his perfect conception in Mary remains always actual. And this conception in her was perfect because it came about in self-dispossesion on behalf of all and in the name of all, and therefore the whole ever was already included.[24]

Mary, the Center and Focus of the Spirit-Enlightened Church

The third moment of the Church's foundation that von Balthasar underlines is Pentecost. In the midst of the Church in prayer, Mary receives the Holy Spirit destined for all.[25] At the event of Pentecost, as innumerable medieval representations portray, she becomes the center and focus of the Spirit-enlightened Church.[26]

Mary's journey in faith, from her overshadowing by the Spirit in Nazareth to the outpouring of the Spirit upon the Church in the Upper Room, is completed in a new role. The

---

23. *Theo-Drama IV*, 395.
24. *Maria und das Priesteramt*, 13.
25. "Maria in der kirchlichen Lehre," 53.
26. *Mary for Today*, 38-39. Cf. *Explorations II: Spouse of the Word*, 177.

Holy Spirit now inspires the Church with her Marian norm.[27]
It is precisely as "full of the Spirit" that she becomes the
Church's model and archetype:

> Henceforth the Church is what was created on the
> cross: the gathering of believers around those who
> have been established in hierarchical offices, with
> Mary in their midst.[28]

Mary prayed with the apostles that what had happened to
her at the annunciation would happen again. At Penetcost, as
the *ecclesia immaculata*, Mary receives the Spirit perfectly so
that she can form the core of the Church along with all saints,
bearers of charisms and all who live this perfect reception of
grace. Her prayer in preparation for Pentecost, in fact, is a
prayer that will be fulfilled many times in history. The essential element communicated by the Spirit is that the Church
live, think and speak from the wellspring of the life of the
Trinity. The primordial word of the new language inculcated
in believers is "Abba" (Rom 8: 15; Gal 4:6).

The Marian Principle, the Sacraments and Charisms

Although we will be returning to these themes, from what
we have seen in this chapter on the origins of the Church in
mystery, we can already say something about how the Marian
principle is vibrantly active in both the sacramental and charismatic realization of the Church.[29] The Marian principle has
to do with the Church's being drawn into the life of the mystery of God that has opened up in the Christ event.

At the eucharist, for instance, the Marian element precedes.
Von Balthasar says that with her perfect yes Mary stands
behind all who participate in the eucharistic celebration and

---

27. *Man in History,* 96ff.
28. *Threefold Garland,* 112.
29. See "Maria in der kirchlichen Lehre," 59ff; *Mary for Today,* 39-40; *Theo-Drama IV,*
    404-405; *Maria und das Priesteramt,* 13.

all who will receive communion. In fact, just before communion we pray, "look not on our sins but on the faith of your Church." At its core, this is Mary's faith and the faith of all who have lived holiness in the Church.

The point here is that the environment of sacramental life in the Church contains as its presupposition the dimension of perfect ecclesial faith. The perfect Marian-ecclesial act of faith completes and perfects what we have done incompletely and imperfectly. We find ourselves in a Spirit-formed and Marian transparency alongside Christ in his reception of life from the Father and response to that gift. This is the sacramentality of lived holiness that shapes our reception and living out of the sacraments.

The other example von Balthasar takes is confession. In this sacrament too we can look to Mary as the one who most opened her soul to God right down to the most hidden corners. Behind everyone who confesses, we have the prototype of the Church in her total transparency before God the Father.[30] On a broader level, and linked to the dynamic patristic notion mentioned in previous chapters, the Marian dimension of the Church is here seen as enfolding us all in the atmosphere of love that facilitates our conversion to God.

In terms of charisms, Mary's yes is repeated throughout the centuries as the inner form of openness to every new outpouring of the Spirit in those charisms which give rise to new communities in the life of the Church. Her yes is that pure openness to the mystery of God in which founders of religious orders or ecclesial movements are molded in order to conform to Christ.[31]

In short, Mary's faith-attitude as the "Servant of the Lord" flows into the Church as her core open availability to God. It is in this openness that the mystery unfolded in Christ continues to become concrete in the Church and the world in each

---

30. See Adrienne von Speyr, *Die Beichte* (Einsiedeln: Johannes Verlag, 1960), espec. 7-8. See also Godfried Cardinal Daneels, "Maria: Disponibilità e atteggiamento di confessione," in Hans Urs von Balthasar (ed.), *La Missione Ecclesiale*, 93-108.
31. See *Die Grossen Ordensregeln*, 14-18.

moment of history. It is made manifest in the existential holiness of life that is a fundamental dimension of the Church's existence and action.

The Church's Marian Principle and Communion
(Spouse of the Word)

In line with contemporary ecclesiology, von Balthasar writes on the Church in terms of a divine-human communion. Mutual love is its norm:

> Born of the utmost love of God for the world, the Church herself is essentially love. What she is, that she ought to be: Her essence is her unique commandment (Jn 15:12). . . . What binds Christians to each other is that they are all brothers and sisters under the same Master (Mt 23:8), all members of the same superlative Head and, following the law of love laid down by that Head, concerned for one another (Rom 12:1; 1 Cor 13; Eph 4:11ff; Col 3:13).[32]

In the foreword to the 1989 edition of *Der Antirömische Affekt,* a work which Peter Henrici comments contains von Balthasar's ecclesiology *in nuce,*[33] Georg Bätzing informs us that from a review of von Balthasar's preparatory notes to this edition it can be seen that he had intended to lay greater emphasis upon the notion of the Church as communion. Already in the first edition of this work, however, he had written of the *Marian* communion of the Church.[34] And that is what we want to look at now.

Reading the birth of the Church in terms of the nuptial categories employed by Paul (Eph 5), von Balthasar often calls the Church *Spouse of the Word.* He links this with theological reflection upon Mary's responsive, "bridal" co-operation and accompaniment of Jesus to the cross. We enter into this *Spouse of*

---

32. *Threefold Garland Paschale,* 134.
33. "A Sketch of von Balthasar's life," 38.
34. *Office of Peter,* 210.

the Word through our yes to Jesus Christ and, in him, our mutual giving to one another in a way modeled on the crucified Christ. But the form of all this is always linked to Mary. She is the mother who generated the Word from whom the Church's communion of mutual love is born:

> The Marian *fiat,* unequalled in its perfection, is the all-inclusive, protective and directive form of all ecclesial life. It is the interior form of *communio,* insofar as this is an unlimited mutual acceptance, far more than a human "getting along together" or fraternization. . . . Thus her attitude becomes foundational for the Church of the faithful, the Church that is pure *communio,* the Church of the "priestly people" who suffer with Jesus Christ.[35]

It is particularly in his reflection on the event of the cross that we see why he views the Marian principle as so central in the Church's communion. It has to do with the encounter of two unities of love being joined into one, forming the true unity-communion of the Church.

On the one hand, the crucified and forsaken Christ contains the divine unity being communicated to us in the Spirit as eucharist and life. Jesus Christ is, of course, as Paul reminds us, also our perfect yes to God (1 Cor 1:19-20). The unity of humankind's responsive yes, however, is not simply absorbed into Jesus' yes. Our autonomy, freedom and dignity is brought into play in the event of redemption. We are to "allow" the event of the cross to happen and to receive Christ's body and Spirit. As such we are to be at once both united with and distinct from Christ.

This is where von Balthasar draws upon the Marian principle. He sees in Mary the unity of humankind summarized in its accompaniment of Christ's self-giving. We are people shaped both in Mary's "letting it be," and in receiving from Jesus Christ all the fruits of his surrendering of himself to the

---

35. *Office of Peter,* 208.

Father. The distinctive nature of humankind's unity through, with and in Christ is represented by Mary.

The Comprehensive Femininity of the Church [36]

It is on the basis of Mary's representative role that von Balthasar writes of a "comprehensive femininity" of the Church. Certainly, the communional experience of the Church as the gathering of the "two or more" is the fruit of the life, death and resurrection of Jesus Christ and the outpouring of the Holy Spirit. In the words of the third century apologist, Lactantius, "God stretched out his arms in his passion and embraced the earth in order to presignify that from the rising of the sun to its setting a future people would be gathered under his wings." But this "future people" formed into a communion of faith, hope and charity, is not merely a distant or inactive beneficiary of the paschal mystery.

We are brought to share in it, here and now, through sacrament and apostolic succession. Moreover, von Balthasar also sees in the presence of Mary, the women and John at the foot of the cross the "Church of love," who actively responds to what is happening at Calvary. She continues as the all-embracing and comprehensive responsive partner:

> The Johannine account brings a mysterious clarification: the presence of a Church of love at the foot of the cross (in contradistinction to the absent Church of office), represented above all by the *Mater dolorosa* and the "disciple whom Jesus loved" to whom he entrusts his mother: a nucleus, here stepping forth into visibility, of the Church which "stands by" the cross, and which afterward (in the question addressed to Peter,

---

36. See "The Mass, a Sacrifice of the Church?" *Explorations III: Creator Spirit,* 185-244. See also *Theo-Drama III,* 281; *New Elucidations,* 187-198; *Short Primer,* 88-96; *Office of Peter,* 183ff; and Georg Bätzing's work, *Die Eucharistie als Opfer der Kirche nach Hans Urs von Balthasar* (Einsiedeln: Johannes Verlag, 1986), espec. 94ff.

Do you love me more than these?) is absorbed into the Petrine Church, there to remain (Jn 21:22ff), despite everything, as a residue inexplicable by Peter and resistant to its own reduction.[37]

From the incarnation to the paschal mystery, the Creator Spirit guides the whole movement of Christ's self-giving. It culminates in the blood and water that flow from the crucified Christ's side, signs of the communication of his life in the Spirit to the Church.[38] Medieval representations were not slow at picking up the theme of Mary's role in the accompaniment and reception of his self-giving. They portrayed Mary with a chalice filled from the wounded side of Christ.

Mary receives the life being communicated and provides a "home" where this life can be safeguarded. Just as at birth Jesus was delivered defenseless to the action and care of his mother (he had to be dressed, carried, fed), now in his death he lets others take care of him and allow himself to be disposed of.

Following on from this, it can be said that the eucharist and the ministerial priesthood find their "home" within this comprehensive femininity of the Church. In other words, Jesus has given himself to us completely in the eucharist; he has made himself food for our nourishment. He has even given away his very act of giving, which is to be continued in the ministerial priesthood. But prior to these fundamental realities in the Church is the Marian "supra-ministerial" bridal response at the cross that continues from generation to generation in all who participate in this:

> He entrusts to her administration not only the fruits of his life and suffering but himself as well. In his passion, he allows himself to be supported by the Father's will, which is expressed concretely in the will of the sinners

---

37. *Mysterium Paschale*, 117. See *Explorations III: Creator Spirit*, 224ff; *Au Coeur du Mystère rédempteur* (Paris: C.L.D., 1980), 53ff. Cf. Adrienne von Speyr, *Geburt der Kirche* (Einsiedeln: Johannes Verlag, 1949); *Allerheiligenbuch I/1*, 40-44, and Albrecht, *Theologie II*, 128-132.

38. Cf. Augustine, *In Jo. tr.* 9, 10 (PL 35:1463-1464); Augustine, *De Gen. ad litt.* 9, c. 19 (PL 34:408); Ambrose, *In Luc. 4, 66* (PL 15:1632).

who "do with him whatever they wish" (Mt 17:12); at the same time, he is sustained by the consent of the feminine Church, suffering with him. So he will be entrusted to the hands of the Church, particularly in his eucharist. Finally, from this center, he will be given into the hands of anyone who becomes a "mother" to him, by doing the will of his Father and allowing him to be born in the world.[39]

There is, therefore, a priority of what might be called the Marian priesthood in the Church. It is noteworthy that in his 1989 edition of *Der antirömische Affekt*, von Balthasar had intended to add a section on the "two priesthoods" in the Church — presumably the "Marian" royal priesthood and the ministerial.[40] Already in the previous edition, he had written:

Christ is entrusted to the hands of Mary at birth and at his death: this is more central than his being given into the hands of the Church in her official, public aspect. The former is the precondition for the latter. Before the masculine, official side appears in the Church, the Church as the woman, the helpmate of the Man, is already there. And it is only possible for the presbyters to exercise their office in the Church of the incarnate, crucified and risen One if they are sustained by the "supra-official" Woman who cherishes and nurtures this official side: for she alone utters the yes that is necessary if the incarnation of the Word is to take place.[41]

Rather than writing of "two priesthoods," it is perhaps more appropriate to write of Christ's one priesthood which the whole Church both benefits from and shares in through ministerial mediation and Marian "supra-ministerial" participation. Mary is not only the model of the common or universal

---

39. *Theo-Drama IV*, 397.
40. See *Der antirömische Affekt* (Einsiedeln: Johannes Verlag, 1989), VII.
41. *Theo-Drama IV*, 397.

priesthood but is at the origin of its dimensions that radiate throughout the whole Church:

> Thus (and only thus) can we say that, in the eucharist, the community is drawn into Christ's sacrifice, offering to God that perfect sacrifice of Head and members which Augustine spoke of in celebrated terms *(De Civ. Dei* X, 6; PL 41:284). Within this perspective, the "common priesthood" of the faithful, with Mary as matrix and archetype, forms the background of the ministerial priesthood; it is the condition that makes the latter possible.[42]

Every celebration of the eucharist is a living participation in the event of Christ's death and resurrection. Inserted into the Marian principle, we all become contemporaries, sharing in Mary's letting the Son give himself up for us and receiving his body and Spirit:

> Everyone who must say, *Nobis quoque peccatoribus,* the *Confiteor* and the *"Domine non sum dignus"* can gather around her [Mary]. In her perfect condition of being the servant, the entire people of God, *simul peccatores et justi,* can take to itself the Body of the Lord and can thereby be mystically incorporated into this Body. In her perfect *fiat,* this people can offer and release the sacrifice for the Church and for the world to the Father. . . . In the New Testament, there is no substitute: if we wish to be redeemed, we must assent to the death of Christ, and then the only thing possible is for the sword that we (as sinners) draw and that (as members of the Church) we allow to take its course at the same time pierces our heart too. But it is only in the Mother that this happens perfectly.[43]

---

42. *Theo-Drama IV,* 398.
43. *Explorations III: Creator Spirit,* 240.

The Communion of Saints

From the time of Origen (c. 185–254) onward, the Church has been described as a communion of saints. Von Balthasar links this reality with Mary also in terms of representation.[44] Formed at the cross as a people of communion, members of Christ's body-bride, we are inserted into a cycle of mutual giving, receiving and handing on with Mary as our prototype.[45]

As a people centered on the dynamic of a mutual being-for-one another, our communion is spiritual and material. We bear one another and are borne by one another. Von Balthasar uses various images in reference to the communion of saints. It is like the circulation of blood in a body (the image used by Paul); an open circle of those who "give without counting the cost"; an overflowing fountain of treasures.

This communion of life where the weak are supported by the strong, where everyone journeys together, is rooted in divine communion. Ecclesial life is already a creaturely participation in the trinitarian mutual-being-for-one-another of the three divine Persons. The communion of saints is linked with the Marian principle in that we participate in the "One Total Christ," as Augustine puts it, by living in a Marian transparency toward God and toward one another. As the one who stood by the cross she "gave" and "received." This principle of giving and receiving continues now within the Marian dynamic of representation on behalf of all. It is in living more and more radically in this reality of the communion of saints that we are to become the heart of the world that will find its fulfillment in heaven.[46]

---

44. See T. Krenski, *Passio Caritatis: Trinitarische Passiologie im Werk Hans Urs von Balthasar* (Einsiedeln: Johannes Verlag, 1990), 292-319.

45. Cf. "Das Katholische an der Kirche," *Kölner Beiträge* 10 (1972), 1-19. Cf. Adrienne von Speyr, *Allerheiligenbuch I/2* (Einsiedeln: Johannes Verlag, 1971), 15-28; Albrecht, *Theologie I*, 251-256; *Theologie II*, 268-282.

46. *Explorations II: Spouse of the Word,* 171.

The Church's Bi-Unity: The Marian and the Petrine Principles

"Reciprocity," "mutual indwelling," *"perichoresis"* "mutual love" are all words that figure in von Balthasar's ecclesiology. But it is in the bi-unity in the Church based on the continuing missions of Mary and Peter that these categories are most evident. There exists a mutual priority of these two principles vis-à-vis each other in the "event" of trinitarian communion becoming history in the Church. A constant theme throughout his writings is how, in many respects, the Marian principle is even more fundamental than the Petrine. This is because the interplay between the various Church principles, charisms and missions all find their embracing point in her.

In this section we shall focus on the relationship between the Petrine and Marian principles. Nowhere is the inseparable link between Trinity, Christology and ecclesiology more evident than in von Balthasar's theology of the inter-relationship of these two aspects of the Church.

We could summarize his line of reasoning as follows: In the Spirit who overshadowed Mary, the Father sent his Son into the world. Through the event of his death and resurrection (an event in which Mary played a major role), the "I" of Christ (who harbors the Father and the Spirit) releases out of himself the mystical body of the Church with many mutually-indwelling personal members, missions and charisms. Their mutual-indwelling (*perichoresis*) is both like and a sharing in God's trinitarian communion.

Just as God is one, so too the Church is one. In that sense, Church unity is what is primary. From the trinitarian perspective, however, the Church is not a monolithic block. Rather, in Jesus Christ, it is what might be called a *perichoretic* unity where there is unity in distinction, communion enriched by differences.

Just as trinitarian love is ordered, so too is the Church as love. As we journey toward our eschatological fulfillment, which has already begun though is not yet complete, the trinitarian-like order of the Church's communion of members and missions revolves particularly around Mary (chronologically and fundamentally the first) and Peter (chosen as first of the apostles and representative of all the apostolic-sacramental line), the Church's two "realsymbols." Everything in the Church is dynamically articulated around Peter and Mary.[47]

"Objective" and "Subjective" Holiness in the Church

In explaining this Peter-Mary nature of the Church, von Balthasar approaches the theme along several lines. One is his consideration of the Church's "objective" and "subjective" holiness.[48] As always, to consider this it is necessary to look at the Christological and trinitarian foundations.

Faith tells us that in God, the third divine Person, the Holy Spirit, is the innermost "subjectivity," freedom and intimacy of mutual love between the Father and the Son. It is precisely as their mutual love in Person that the Holy Spirit is also the "objective" expression or personification of this mutual love.

To explain this further and adopting the helpful although not perfect analogy proposed by some Church Fathers, von Balthasar takes the case of the marriage union between two partners and their child. A child is the "objective" fruit and measure of the parents' "subjective" mutual love. Somewhat analogously, in God, the fruitfulness of the mutual love between the Father and the Son is a Person, who is eternally the "objective" witness to and constant igniter of the ever new "subjective" love between them.

In coming, out of love, to reconcile the world with God, the Son of God liberated us by taking our place. He gave himself up for us, and drew us into the divine, trinitarian life. Entering

---

47. See *Christen sind einfältig* (Einsiedeln: Johannes Verlag, 1983), 65-68, espec. 68. See also *Razing the Bastions*, 39ff; *Explorations II: Spouse of the Word*, 157ff; *Explorations III: Creator Spirit*, 238ff; *Glory of the Lord I*, 556-570; *Office of Peter*, 183ff; 204ff; 290ff.
48. See *Theologik III*, 282-380.

into our need to conquer freedom, the Son of God "emptied" himself of his divinity (*kenosis,* Phil 2:6-11). As God, Jesus certainly obeys the Father in the Spirit-love that the Father shows him. But as man, this love takes the form of mandate-obedience.

Jesus says "not my will but yours be done" and, in our sinful condition, he experiences the Spirit as rule, as a divine plan which must be obeyed, one to which he must bring his human will into conformity. In what von Balthasar calls a "trinitarian inversion," the Son lets the "objective" and "norm" dimension of the Spirit take the lead as it were. Of course, the Spirit is doing no more than mediating what all three from eternity have determined out of love for us.

After his death and resurrection, in the wake of the "accomplishment" (Jn 19:30) of his mission and the breathing-forth of the Spirit of mission on the cross (Mk 15:37; Lk 23:46; Mt 27:50), the risen Christ breathed out the Spirit not only to the Father but upon the Church and the world. This Holy Spirit, as Irenaeus writes, continually rejuvenates the churchly vessel, which contains the eternally young presence of Christ.

Now, within history, there is a people that has been brought to share in the very intimacy of the mutual love between the Father and Son. This is the goal of the incarnation. As Christ's "other self," his bride-body, we are called to live a life "in the Spirit," sharing in the "subjective" holiness of mutual love found in the very life of God.

The important point for von Balthasar is that the Spirit given after Easter remains undeniably linked to the fact that "Jesus Christ has come in the flesh" (1 Jn 4:2). Just as it was in the life of Christ, so too the Spirit will always be pointing us to the objective norm of the Father's will. The Spirit-guided Church can never be separated from the incarnational dynamism of ecclesial life. As people who are journeying toward our ultimate fulfillment in heaven, for now the "objective" dimension of the Spirit appears to us as rule and norm. But it is to ensure that we do not propose our own human spirit as the Holy Spirit that the Church's "objectified" rule and elements of holiness form us. It opens us up to transcend our personal plans for the sake of the trinitarian dimensions revealed to us in the paschal mystery. All of this comes from love and invites us to love.

Institution and Charism

As well as writing about the Peter-Mary dimensions of the Church in terms of the "objective-subjective" polarity of the Church's holiness, another avenue von Balthasar pursues is to employ the categories of institution and charism. The "objective" dimension of the Spirit is the hierarchical, sacramental and institutional side of the Church, linked by von Balthasar with the office of Peter. Mary, the woman, overshadowed by the Holy Spirit, is intimately linked to the charismatic dimension of the Church.

The institutional principle can be understood as a guaranteed "crystallization of love"[49] found in the preaching of the word, the tradition, the sacraments, the hierarchy and other ecclesial elements such as canon law. Terms such as *sacred* scripture, *holy* sacraments, the *Holy* Father carry the meaning of holiness in this objective sense. Unlike Tertullian, Joachim of Fiore, and others, von Balthasar reaffirms the institutional element of the Church as an original constitutive dimension and not some structure added later. The Church's unity is not made by us, but rather by the Spirit working among us in these tangible means.

Nevertheless, the Church's unity is articulated also in terms of the believers' mutual love in the body of Christ in its openness to the Spirit. The goal of the sacramental and institutional dimension in the Church is to form a people who share in the "subjective" aspect of the Spirit as the mutual love between the Son and the Father. This is what Jesus came to

---

49. *Explorations II: Spouse of the Word*, 26, 34; *Explorations III: Creator Spirit*, 501; Cf. Kehl, *Kirche als Institution*, 200-301.

communicate. And it is this which Mary, in particular, shares in. The annunciation, the cross and Pentecost all point to Mary's reception of this great gift of the Spirit.

The Marian principle in the Church is her "subjective" holiness not merely in terms of being formed by the institution but also in terms of existential freedom in the Spirit, and inspirations or charisms "from above." The Spirit is not only "norm" but also freedom. Mary's pure and free, living and responsive yes echoes throughout the mystical body as a living reception of the Spirit, response to Christ and immersion in the bosom of the Father at the heart of the Church's communion.

Formed in Christ through the elements of "objective holiness," what God wants is our sanctification in terms of existential holiness. Through his death and resurrection, the risen Christ breathes forth the Spirit upon us also in the form of existential holiness, freedom and inspiration. Meditating on Mary's special link with the Spirit, von Balthasar glimpses the Church's Marian principle very clearly in the charismatic dimension of the Church.

The great charismatic "mystics," especially the founders of new religious families or people with deep intuitions for the Church — Origen, Basil, Augustine, Benedict, Hildegaard, the two Mathildes, Julian of Norwich, Ignatius of Loyola, John of the Cross, Teresa of Avila — are manifestations of the Church's "Marian" charismatic profile.[50] They bear witness to the freedom of forms of Church life. These ever new forms emerge from the inspirations and missions from the Spirit that are pouring out in the midst of the existential Marian holiness.

Accordingly, von Balthasar writes that the Holy Spirit appears in the Church both as institution and gift or charism. Institution *and* charism, rule *and* inspiration go together:

> We can say that the Holy Spirit always lives in the Church as objective as well as subjective Spirit: as institution, or rule, or *disciplina,* and as inspiration and loving obedience to the Father in this spirit of adop-

---

50. *Theologik III,* 291-293.

tion. . . . Certainly, "when Christ our life appears, you
will also appear with him in glory" (Col 3:3-4). And
then the institutional aspect of the Church will disappear in the same way as it did for the risen Lord and
take on the aspect of the adoption of God's children.
For then we will no longer need to learn obedience but
will have it by instinct and as part of our freedom, and
the Spirit will tower over us objectively only in his
divine original meaning — as witness and igniter of
love.[51]

Church institution and charism, office and holiness are
inseparably united in the same origin and goal. There is a reciprocity of life between them allowing the Christ "event" to
become history in each new generation. It is in their inter-
action that the Church remains constantly young:

Neither aspect can be renounced but must be continually fitted to the other in mutual harmony. There are
sides of the external discipline that must be revived,
perhaps even restored, by an inner inspiration. But
there is also much in the same external form that
would be sufficiently living and vital to free up true
inner inspiration if one only had the desire to see it as
the Holy Spirit presents it, undistorted by the optical
lenses through which one normally sees externals.[52]

The Inter-Relationship of Mary and Peter

No matter what terms he uses to explain his meaning (objective holiness/subjective holiness and institution/charism),
von Balthasar seems to prefer to speak simply of "Peter" and
"Mary." Other categories seem too restrictive for what he
wants to express. One reason for this is his personalist

---

51. *Explorations IV: Spirit and Institution*, 239.
52. *Explorations IV: Spirit and Institution*, 241.

ecclesiology — he sees everything in the Church as linked to persons.

By referring to these two polyvalent "realsymbols," he also manages to give a living expression to the two co-essential dimensions which expand right through the Church. Although a great admirer of Yves Congar's work, von Balthasar feels uneasy with the way Congar opposes life and structure or charism and institution. For von Balthasar the Church, living and official, is one single living Spirit-enlightened body. He compares it to the human organism whose bones too are alive and indispensable; otherwise we could not stand straight and carry out an infinite variety of free movements.[53]

But how do the two principles (Mary and Peter) inter-relate? It is not a question of quantitative measure. Nor is it an either-or situation. A guiding phrase can be found in the words of Paul that the Church of Christ is founded on "the apostles and the prophets" (Eph 2:20). With the Holy Spirit as their true point of convergence, in Christ both principles are coextensive with the Church. With the Trinity as the ultimate horizon to explain their inter-relationship, mutual love is always the norm of norms.

Von Balthasar quotes Laurentin, Journet and the Vatican Councils I and II to say: "The entire Church is priestly; the entire Church is Marian" and "the entire Church is Petrine, the entire Church is Marian."[54] The two aspects of the Church move toward one another in reciprocity in order to become one Church of Christ. In mutually indwelling one another (*perichoresis*) the Marian and Petrine principles point beyond themselves to the transcending unity of Christ:

> What is important is to see not that but *how* the two aspects of the Church inter-relate in order to become one Church of Christ as body and as bride. This move-

---

53. See *Test Everything*, 65.
54. *Office of Peter*, 205; *Theologik III*, 287. Cf. *L'église du Verbe Incarné, Vol. II: Sa structure interne et son unité catholique* (Paris: Desclée de Brouwer, 1951), espec. 393-452, and the Vatican Councils I and II, which contend that the entire Church is Petrine in that Peter and his successors represent the Church personally (See D'Avanzo at Vatican I, *Mansi* 52, 762).

ment is not symmetric. All objective holiness subsists out of love for the subjective movement of members of the Church toward the holiness of Christ in the Holy Spirit. The perfect subjective holiness (in Mary) is, on the one hand, presupposed for the very life of Christ himself and, on the other hand, she is "mother" (cf. Rv 12:17) of the whole subjective-objective Church, therefore also of the ministerial aspect and the sacraments founded by Christ. To repeat once again, it is in this movement that the identity of the one Holy Spirit in his double aspect is revealed.[55]

Writing in metaphoric mode, and resonating with trinitarian motifs, von Balthasar speaks of Peter in Mary and Mary in Peter. From his writings, however, we can outline five points that he offers for reflection upon how in "the kingdom of mutual love that is the Church everything is in constant movement between these two principles."[56] While outlining these, it is worth noting that we will also come back to this in the next part of the book when we look at some of the more concrete dimensions of the Marian principle.

Firstly, the whole tendency of the Christian faith is incarnational. The Church is never meant to be an abstraction from this world. Since the Church as bride of Christ is the extension and product of the living reality of Christ, an essential structure is needed to keep it such. And this comes in the form of sacraments and ministry founded by the bridegroom Christ. Life and form are inseparable elements in the whole life of the Church.

Secondly, institution is the condition of possibility for the continuing realization of the nuptial dialogue-event between Mary-Church and Christ throughout history. Through the institution we are guaranteed the possibility of participating in the original event of the Church's birth from Christ at any and every time. Christ the head continues to be present to his

---

55. *Theologik III*, 289-290.
56. *Christen sind einfältig*, 68. For the following see especially *Theo-Drama III*, 353-360.

(Marian) body-bride, making her fruitful, giving life through the distribution of sacraments and ministry.

The office instituted by Christ imparts to the Church her life-giving substance (in the eucharist) and the word of forgiveness (in sacramental absolution). The Marian "bridal" dimension is the responsive element of the dialogue-relationship with Christ from whose well-springs the Church continually receives her being and life. Accordingly, the Marian principle is manifest in the existential manifestations of the dialogue with the Church's spouse. The new forms of ecclesial life and spirituality that emerge in various eras of our history are examples of this. Ultimately, it is the degree of participation in the nuptial encounter itself that will remain for us in paradise. The institutional will not remain:[57]

> The whole structural aspect of the Church is also mediating and instrumental. . . . Much in these institutions is, in the deepest sense, conditioned by time and disappears when fulfillment is reached in the next world. This is the case with the official, hierarchic structure of the Church and her individual sacraments and also with certain provisional forms of the life of grace they impart. . . . What never falls away is the nuptial encounter between God and the creature, for whose sake the framework of the structures is now set up and will later be dismantled. This encounter, therefore, must be the real core of the Church. The structure and the graces they impart are what raise the created subjects up to what they should be in God's design: a humanity formed as a bride to the Son, become the Church.[58]

Thirdly, the institution provides an objective "rule" we can live under. In other words, since we have not yet reached perfection in love, we need to be formed by the "rule" aspect of the Holy Spirit in the institution. What may at times seem harsh to us is, in fact, a dimension of divine love freeing us and

---

57. Cf. *Explorations IV: Spirit and Institution*, 239.
58. *Explorations II: Spouse of the Word*, 158.

extending us to be fully human as a gift of ourselves, in God, to God and to others. It is a fashioning into the Church's perfect Marian core of holiness. Of course, office holders themselves must acquire an "advance installment" of subjective love in order to carry out their office.

Fourthly, the Marian and Petrine principles are both involved in our education in love, in our formation to the mind of Christ. As well as being a "rule," the institution is a pedagogical instrument. It forms an *anima ecclesiastica* within us that becomes a sharing in the wisdom of *the Anima ecclesiastica,* namely, Mary the Seat of Wisdom:

> The redemptive events of the incarnation, culminating in the cross, have freed us from the bonds of sin; and the Spirit whom Christ sent down upon the Church at Pentecost, from the Father, is the Spirit of freedom and sonship: this Spirit impels the believer toward the full, Marian yes. Nonetheless, the fact that we have been "called to freedom" (Gal 5:13) means that we have been called to follow Christ: set free on the basis of the cross, we are pointed in the direction of the cross, to a new form of service (Rom 6:18ff). This applies not only to the imperfect members of the Church who are to be educated toward perfect love by the Church's officeholders; it applies to the entire Church in her Marian perfection. . . . It also follows, however, that those who have been formed by the Church's ministry and discipline, by Christ's authority, are thus initiated into the mind of Christ; they have truly come of age in a Christian sense; this gives them an existential knowledge of Christian truth that is equal to that possessed by the Church in her official representatives. Perfect holiness is also wisdom; it is Mary, not Peter, who is called "Seat of Wisdom." The Church is the "Bride" of Christ, and at the same time she is equipped with an official and institutional side:

in this intertwining relationship lies the Church's inner, dramatic constitution.[59]

Fifthly, von Balthasar writes of the inter-relating of these principles in the living, guarding and making explicit of the prophetic sense of believers' faith. Here he notes a "tension" in the reciprocity between what Newman calls the episcopal ministry and the prophetic ministry of the Church. The episcopal dimension guards the authenticity of the prophetic sense of the believers' living faith, while the prophetic ministry of the universal Marian Church can enlighten the episcopal ministry.

The point here is that charisms, inspirations or intuitions associated with the Marian principle pour forth from the Spirit not through the hierarchy alone but through the Spirit's gift of holiness also in the midst of the non-ministerial aspect of the Church. While the Marian principle can never be isolated from the hierarchical principle in the Church (with its charism of discernment), nevertheless it provides insights, directions, new forms of life that deserve to be appreciated:

> The hierarchy whose role it is in particular to discern spirits, must be aware that the novelties willed and guided by the Spirit only in rare cases come from the hierarchy within the Church, rather they flower from the ranks of non-ministerial believers. . . . The charism of the great popes and bishops was directed toward the re-building of the Church or the diocese overall . . . to establish new religious families for the most part is not their role. Just how much such communities that blossom in the Spirit can be put to use by them for the great tasks of sanctification and mission can be seen in the examples that are well known by all.[60]

Clearly, there is going to be a certain "tension" between the Petrine and Marian principles. But it is a creative one, leading

---

59. *Theo-Drama III*, 357-358.
60. *Theologik III*, 292-293.

the Church to be fully as Christ wants her to be. Commenting on this relationship, von Balthasar refers to Newman:

> Finally this can be explained by reference to the tension between the "episcopal" and the "prophetical" office, as set forth by Newman. Tradition and the instinct of faith are of the essence of the whole (Marian-Petrine) Church. But the episcopal office has to guard the authenticity of the "prophetical" sense of faith that is alive in the whole people; it must evaluate it and keep it pure. On the other hand, the episcopal office, for that very reason, has to pay attention to this "prophetical" office of the whole Church, and when necessary it must learn from it (as when the Beloved Disciple tells Peter, "It is the Lord," Jn 21:7). For Newman, on his journey toward the Catholic Church, had a crucial insight: during the Arian crisis of the fourth century, while a number of holy bishops did put forward the orthodox position, it was primarily the ordinary faithful, rather than the episcopate, who proclaimed and maintained the divine tradition entrusted to the infallible Church.[61]

Von Balthasar gives a concrete example of the interplay between these two principles. He believes that the very process of coming to formulate the Marian dogmas of the Immaculate Conception and Assumption shows the interlinking of the immaculate, indefectible and infallible dimensions of the Church. The enquiries of both Pius IX and XII at the time of the declaration of those dogmas manifests the Spirit-led sense of the faithful (*sensus fidelium*) as an expression of a Marian "feeling with" and "being of one mind" with the Petrine principle. The Marian principle belongs together in *consensus* with the Petrine as a point of reference for orthodox faith. Indeed, von Balthasar speaks of an "infallibility" or indefectibility attached to the *sensus fidelium,* understood not in terms

---

61. *Theo-Drama III*, 358.

of democracy, but rather in its rootedness in Mary's immaculate yes.[62]

This bipolar character of the Church's life revolving around
Marian subjective, holiness and Petrine, objective holiness
constitutes her irreducible, inner dramatic tension. It is in this
tension that the Church as the extension of Christ ("body") as
well as his partner ("bride") participates in Christ's redemptive mission and, undergirding this, in his trinitarian being.[63]
There is a mutually enriching aspect in this interplay of light
and life:

> There is drama in the encounter between the believer's
> experiential knowledge, which comes from the fullness
> of Christ, and authority's official knowledge, which is
> imparted by Christ directly. These two modes of
> knowledge mutually presuppose each other. Thus
> Mary, the *ecclesial immaculata* is on the scene prior to
> the call of the Apostles, yet the concrete community is
> built on the "rock" of the apostolate; again, Peter's
> avowal of love ("Do you love me more than these?")
> presupposes an "advance installment" of love on the
> part of the Marian-Johannine Church. This "advance
> installment" remains a permanent feature insofar as
> the official Church has to initiate the community into
> love, which is only possible, generally speaking, if this
> institutional side of the Chuch itself possesses love.[64]

Uniting the Principles — the Papacy and Marian Transparency

Before concluding this section, it is necessary to look briefly
at von Balthasar's contention that the fruit of Vatican II's

---

62. "Das katholische an der Kirche," 12. See also *Office of Peter*, 212ff. Cf. *Explorations II: Spouse of the Word*, 162.
63. "Das katholische der Kirche," 12.
64. *Theo-Drama III*, 358-359.

ecclesiology is that the papacy finds its "home" within the Marian principle. The whole objective-institutional dimension of the Church finds personal expression in the figure of Peter. But to carry out his role of unity and setting others free for service in their special mission, the role of the Marian principle is essential.

As the "outward" principle of unity, the pope's role is "an impossibility," made possible only by God's will in creating him. As the "fatherly head" of the Church, he is the one called to "love more"; his role is "excentric" in that he is to care for the periphery within the communion of the Church; he has judicial authority rooted in the office of judge that Christ received from the Father, an office exercised in order to seek reconciliation and unity. And since the Petrine office cares for the periphery, it manifests itself as infallible.

How is Peter to carry out his role?

Von Balthasar replies by referring to the Fathers' saying about Mary and Jesus, namely, *femina circumdabit virum* (woman will surround/protect man) (Jer 31:22, LXX).[65] The office of Peter is not to be trapped in a pyramid-like isolation.[66] In fact, von Balthasar notes that, starting with the disintegration of the Holy Roman Empire, there is a movement toward the re-integration of the pope within what he calls the "apostolic foursome" of Peter, John, Paul and James. This movement found its key in Vatican II with the clearer emergence of the Marian profile of the Church.

It seems that in adopting Yves Congar's notion of catholicity as the Church's universal capacity for unity, and his understanding of the dynamic universality of the principles which yield her unity, von Balthasar wants to highlight the central feature of Mary as the internal point of this unity.[67] All the principles of the Church that we introduced in chapter 2 find

---

65. *Explorations II: Spouse of the Word*, 165; *Office of Peter*, 205ff.
66. *Office of Peter*, 21ff. See Hermann Pottmeyer, *Towards a Papacy in Communion* (New York: Crossroad, 1998).
67. "Conscience de la catholicité," in Yves Congar, *Esquisse du mystère de l'église* (Paris, 1953) referred to in *Office of Peter*, 323. Cf. "Das Katholische an der Kirche," *Kölner Beiträge* 10 (1972), 1-19.

their place to the degree they share in the Marian transparency to Christ. Each principle shares in the whole of the Church, and each one thereby shares in each other. Recounting a conversation with von Balthasar on the topic of the Church's profiles, Marisa Cerini recalls his response:

> As I see it — he said — just like Mary and her ecclesial dimension, the four members each represent a fundamental dimension of the Church: Peter represents "ministry," John "love," Paul "novelty" and "freedom in the Spirit," James, bishop of Jerusalem after Peter's departure, "tradition" and "fidelity to the tradition."
> At that point he drew a shape on the chalkboard distributing each of these in four different points in the shape of a cross — Peter to the right, John to the left, James above and Paul below. He then traced an ellipse around them by way of indicating Mary who embraces everyone.[68]

The ontology of the Church is such that there is a mutual indwelling (circumincession) in Mary of the Church's principles, dimensions and states of life.[69] If any one of the four major principles should be separated or made absolute, the Marian profile of the Church would suffer.

If, for instance, the Jacobine element of law and tradition is one-sidedly emphasized, we end up with positivism and integralism, a reactionary clinging to obsolete forms.

Should the Petrine-institutional dimension loom large, the Church's visage becomes distorted in organization and administration.

If the Pauline characteristic of freedom in the Spirit is unilaterally highlighted, the result is rationalism and dogmaticism, a diplomatic updating following what is popular and fashionable.

Finally, an excess on the part of the Johannine principle flows into Gnosticism, pneumatism and love as "experience,"

---

68. Marisa Cerini, "Dimensione mariana" in *Unità e Carismi* 8(1998)/1, 2-4.
69. See *Explorations I: The Word Made Flesh*, 223.

mere universal humanitarian kindness focusing on a change in social structures.

So there is a permanent "tension" in the life of the Church: office, love, tradition and newness are four principles which are difficult to unite. But this is precisely the work of Mary in all of this. If Mary, overshadowed by the Spirit, is the creaturely place where we see the trinitarian God turning toward the world, and his self-revelation precisely as Trinity, then the vocation of the Church is to be the Marian sphere where we see an articulation of the various principles of Church's life in a manner analogous to the trinitarian life.

Accordingly, reading the global picture of Vatican II ecclesiology, von Balthasar sees it as indicating how Peter's office, established clearly in Vatican I, is to manifest its function in the heart of the Marian *communio* and the *collegium* of bishops. The Marian principle is the liberating embrace of this Petrine ministry.

> Not only did the Marian yes precede the incarnation of the Church's Head (and hence of her members), whereas the appointment of the Twelve under the leadership of Peter is a single act — thought weighty in its consequences — on the part of Jesus; qualitatively the form of the Marian faith (consenting to God's activity) is offered to the *Catholica* as the model of all being and acting.[70]

Even Peter's infallibility is rooted in Mary's perfect yes to God. The Marian "letting be," and so "setting free," exercises a formative influence on the official, Petrine universality, which has the task of "holding together" and "administering" and thus cannot "let be" in the same sense.[71] The deficiency of the office-holders in the Church is covered by the Marian immaculate Church.[72] And so von Balthasar writes that it is centrally right if the fatherly head of the Church turns again and again

---

70. *Office of Peter*, 206.
71. *Office of Peter*, 206.
72. *Maria und das Priesteramt*, 15.

to the mother of the Church, to ask for her assistance and fruit-fulness in his ministerial work.[73]

The successor of Peter can always find new strength for witness in a Church of Mary.[74] And this, not merely in a devotional sense, but in openness to what the Spirit is saying to the Church through those endowed with charisms or missions:

> Peter and all the other official ministers must always listen to the Spirit working and creating in the Marian Church, and also obey him who speaks through the saints and true bearers of charisms.[75]

The Marian and Johannine Principles

Consideration of the Marian principle and the Church's communion would not be complete without further reference to the Johannine principle. John 19:25-27 presents the scene of Mary and John at the foot of the cross. It is the Church's "foundation document,"[76] because they represent the new community formed at the cross. It is significant that von Balthasar points also to the Mary-John relationship as an "original cell" of the Church.

He sees in the Mary-John relationship something of a discovery of the "sacramentality" of the presence of God in each neighbor and the "sacramentality" of the presence of Christ in the "two or more gathered in his name" (Mt 18:20). Mary and John form the new community where, through his death and resurrection, the visible presence of Christ on earth is now to be found invisibly among those who are gathered in his name. Everything which forms the organism of the Church will come from this:[77]

---

73. *Maria und das Priesteramt,* 15

74. *Mary for Today,* 20.

75. "Das katholische an der Kirche," 17.

76. *Threefold Garland,* 103.

77. *Mary for Today,* 53. See also, Adrienne von Speyr, *Johannes IV: Geburt der Kirche* (Einsiedeln: Johannes Verlag, 1949).

In them is to be portrayed visibly and in a manner appropriate to their state of life the transformation of the visible presence of Christ on earth into his invisible presence wherever two or three are gathered together in his name. They are to prove to all ages that Christianity is possible: that we can truly find God whom we love in the neighbor whom we love without thereby jeopardizing the absoluteness of our love for God by the love we are to have for our fellow man. For this turning to the neighbor is more than just a command of God. The divine Son and Friend lives so truly in the neighbor that it is henceforth possible to seek and find him wholly in one's neighbor.[78]

On the one hand, in giving Mary to the care of the apostle John, Jesus gives the Church the gift of the center and highpoint, which personifies the immaculate and unconditional yes of humanity to all of God's plan of salvation for the world. On the other hand, John represents the link with the hierachical dimension of the Church which receives Mary. He mediates between Peter and Mary. By taking Mary home, writes von Balthasar, the heavenly Church who has been perfected in advance, is infused into the form of the earthly, organized Church, and this latter must care for and protect the purity and sanctity of the original, ideal Church.

The Marian-Johannine link is so strong in von Balthasar's writings that it is difficult at times to distinguish between John's principle of love and Mary's nuptial-maternal unifying love.[79] He writes of John having had maternal care toward the principle which Peter represents. John highlights Peter's office and lovingly accompanies it.

As we draw this chapter to a close, we can conclude with a citation that indicates von Balthasar's "trinitarian thinking" of the Church as a communion. Mary, Peter and John interrelate in a mutual reciprocity. Each is in a certain sense

---

78. *Christian State of Life,* 210.
79. See, for example, *Maria und das Priesteramt,* 14-16.

"center" of the ecclesial realm. What we have tried to indicate in this section was how this is the case in terms of the Marian principle:

> But with Mary, John too must come forward in the Church. He takes his place at a strangely veiled mid-point exposed to all winds, between Peter, to whom he is united by mission and apostolate, and Mary, to whom he is united both by the commission to love given under the cross and by that pure love of the Lord that is not to be exhausted in any one form. With one hand in Peter's and the other in Mary's he unites Mary and Peter in terms of their mission. (This does not prevent Mary, as *Ekklesia* from being the higher midpoint between both apostles, nor Peter from remaining the visible midpoint as the one who administers everything, including love, including Mary.)[80]

---

80. *Razing the Bastions*, 41.

The Church's Marian Principle and Mission
(Mother of God and Mother of the Church)

At the Council of Ephesus (431) Mary was called the Mother of God (*Theotokos*). It is a title that takes up Luke's description of Mary as "Mother of the Lord" (Lk 1:43). Already in the third century this title was attributed to her in Egypt.[81] From it we can appreciate that the maternal dimension of Mary's archetypal faith is both unique and highly significant. If this aspect of Mary's faith experience is as a maternal principle in the Church and a maternal profile of the Church, its implications are vast. In his writings, von Balthasar invites us to recapture the centrality of this theme.[82] Not least because it is linked to the very missionary dynamism of the Church, whose outreach is nothing less than all of humanity and the cosmos itself. This provides us with the focus for this final chapter of part 4.

Before proceeding, let us note how von Balthasar links Mary's maternity and the Holy Spirit very closely. This is not surprising, since the Holy Spirit, the bond of mutual love in the Trinity, is the divine locus in which the divine and human are constantly meeting. He describes this encounter as a movement of upward-thrusting buds opening in the light that comes from "above":

> Since the Holy Spirit proceeds from the Father who created the world and the Son who redeemed it, he is the divine locus of the unity of the order of nature and the order of grace, and in the freedom in which he blows he is the locus of the ever-new transpositions of the one order into the other, in such a way that the au-

---

81. See Gabriele Giamberardini, *Il culto mariano in Egitto,* 3 vols. (Jerusalem: Franciscan Printing Press, 1974-1978).
82. See *Office of Peter,* 183ff.

tonomy of each order is not compromised. The order of nature is not closed in upon itself, because the Father created all things for the Son; nor is the order of grace closed in upon itself, because the Son became man in order to redeem the entire world and bring it back to the Father, "so that God may be all in all" (1 Cor 15:24, 28). The natures of the world are broken open in order that they may be perfected in God's own life, but God has poured himself out in order to drench the world with his eternal love. The upward-thrusting bud must therefore be placed again and again in the light that falls from above, since it can open up only in this light; and the light must be directed again and again downward into the darknesses of the world, so that it may awaken the definitive life there.[83]

This movement between heaven and earth, guided by the Spirit, is explained by von Balthasar as a perfecting and extension of the "event" of communion between Christ and his Church gathered around Mary. Entering into this ever new "event," Christians find themselves in the midst of a divine adventure:

It is the one who gives the Bride away, the Holy Spirit, who directs this movement of heaven and earth in love, perfecting thus the relationship that was entered into in Christ with the Bride Sion-Mary-Ecclesia. Christians live in the epicenter of this event, which wishes to become reality in them too, and for them, through the gift they make of their own life to love. Their existence is to be an ever-creative translation in the Holy Spirit, an ever-new future of God.[84]

It was the Creator Spirit (the One who "gave the Bride away") who formed Mary's response at the annunciation when she became mother of Christ. Through the event of

---

83. *Explorations III: Creator Spirit,* 387.
84. *Explorations III: Creator Spirit,* 387.

Christ's death on the cross, the Spirit formed the virgin Mary in a new maternity of his mystical body. Since Pentecost, the Holy Spirit has fused the maternity of his vessel (Mary) into the Church. Now it continues to be the Spirit who maintains the Church in her exclusive Marian-bridal response to Christ and her universal Marian-maternal outreach to the world. The Holy Spirit is the point of convergence between the institutional and charismatic-Marian dimensions of the Church.

It was through the Holy Spirit that the *inner* trinitarian Son-Father relationship turned *outward* in the Christ-world mission. In some analagous fashion, it is the Holy Spirit, the bond of unity in distinction, who explains how the Church can contemporaneously be (Mary) the Bride turned toward the Bridegroom and, in imitation of Christ's universal outreach, Virgin-Mother open to everyone, including sinners.[85] It is through the Holy Spirit's action that Mary's "office" is one of virgin-bridal-motherhood in the ecclesial "cosmos of grace":[86]

> Mary, in giving birth spiritually and physically to the Son, becomes the universal Mother of all believers, for the Church as body is born of Christ and is herself Christ. Mary is the prototype of the Church, not only because of her virginal faith but also equally because of her fruitfulness. This is, indeed, not autonomous (as that of the goddesses of fertility) but wholly ancillary, since it is Christ, not Mary, who brought the Church into being by his passion. All the same, she took part, as an intermediary, in this creation by the universality and unrestrictedness of her *fiat,* which the Son is able to use as an infinitely plastic medium to bring forth from it new believers, those born again. Her presence with him at the cross, her agreement to his abandonment of her to the Church in the midst of his dereliction on the cross, her eternal role as the woman in labor (Rv 12), show how fully her self-surrender is uni-

---

85. *Explorations III: Creator Spirit,* 113.
86. "Die Erscheinung," 75.

versalized to become the common source, the produc-
tive womb, of all Christian grace.[87]

The Apocalyptic Image of the Woman in the Wilderness

As we have already seen, the Book of Revelation, especially
chapter 12 with its depiction of the woman crying out in travail, provides von Balthasar with a starting point for his reflection on the continuing maternity *of* and *within* the Church
expressed in the Marian principle.[88] The scene shows that she
who has reached the ultimate state envisaged for creation is
endowed with insignia of "incomparable motherhood." She is
clothed with the sun, with the moon under her feet, and
crowned with the twelve stars of the Lamb. It is as one
immersed in the Christological interpenetration of heaven
and earth, that she dwells at the heart of the Church:

> At the heart of the Church, however, stands Mary, and
> what applies to her Son's eucharist applies analo-
> gously to her: it is not that she is either in heaven or on
> earth, but she is earth lifted up into heaven and heaven
> turned toward earth. Nor is there anything strained
> here: it is all perfectly natural, for this is how the crea-
> ture's ultimate state was envisaged.[89]

The world is now in the time of choice. After Jesus' death
and resurrection what von Balthasar calls the "Theodrama"
(God's redemptive action on us, for us, with us) has entered an
ever more intense phase. The choice facing us has become
clearer — to say yes or no to the risen Christ. In this phase of
salvation history, Mary is transferred for the remaining
earth-time to what the imagery of the Book of Revelation calls
the "wilderness" or "desert." The "desert" is the place of

---

87. *Explorations II: Spouse of the Word,* 165-166.
88. For this section see, "Die Erscheinung"; *Mary for Today,* 7ff; *Theo-Drama III,* 334ff;
    Theo-Drama IV, 464f.
89. *You Crown the Year,* 199.

impoverishment and distress on the one hand, but also a place of rejuvenation, of concentrated attention to God.

In this desert Mary remains what she was and will be for all eternity: the mother. This mother gives Christ to the Church and the world "not just at one single moment in history but at every moment of the history of the Church and of the world."[90] In doing this, Mary makes her own the prayer and activity of the Church. This gives confidence in the face of trials. No matter what difficulties come (nowhere can one evade the "rage of the dragon against the woman" and his war "with the rest of her offspring," the Christians), this woman is nourished through world-time with manna from on high, which keeps her alive and makes her fruitful: the victory of Christ will be hers.

But how and where is this Marian principle operative? Is Mary's place "u-topic"? At this point we need to recall von Balthasar's own admonition not to reduce consideration of Mary's role to devotional piety. She has a social-ecclesial personality. Accordingly, while from the world's point of view the Woman remains u-topian and without "form," something of her invisible form is discernible in her genuine children.[91] In them the invisible realities become visible. Mary continues, as it were, where people become "mothers" of Christ.

The operation of the Marian principle is to be seen therefore in the woman's children, who wage war by keeping the commandment of love, wielding the weapons of love, above all the Word (Rv 1:16; 19:15; Mt 10:34; Heb 4:12). It is to be seen in the maternity of holiness in the Church. And this is a reason for Christian hope. Ultimately, no matter how bad things become, the Church is not affected in its feminine core of existential holiness by the power of the dragon. It is within this, writes von Balthasar, that the rock of Peter is safeguarded and gains new energy.[92]

---

90. *Mary for Today*, 40.
91. *Theo-Drama IV*, 468.
92. Cf. *Mary for Today*, 19.

In one of those stimulating intuitions that he opens up without pursuing them, von Balthasar unites the Church, the apocalyptic cry of the *mater dolorissima* (Rv 12) that continues to the end of the world, and the groaning of the Holy Spirit in the innermost heart of the tragedy of the sinful world (Rom 8).[93] The Holy Spirit who "sighs" experiences the hopelessness of the world; in experiencing it together with us, the Spirit gives it a place in the wordless sighs of dialogue found in inner-trinitarian "prayer."[94] The yearning for fullness running throughout creation is also linked with the woman of sorrows, the woman who knows how to love and how to suffer in giving birth to Christ. As co-empowering factors both Mary and the Spirit are intimately linked in the creation of a new humanity in the crucified and risen Christ.

Under Mary's Mantle

The fruitful and apostolic character of love led the German mystics to employ the image of the mantle of Mary. It is an image to which von Balthasar refers approvingly.[95] It is apt for expressing how the whole range of the Church, the perfect, the advancing, and the beginners are all gathered together beneath a mantle that covers all her progeny. We shelter under Mary's mantle and under the "smaller" cloaks of the saints that are so much an expression of the Marian principle in the Church.[96] This mantle forms the very fabric of the Church's maternity.

The key here is Mary's unique maternal solidarity with us. Only sin allows for a "private" mentality and a lack of communion of which Mary's immaculate love knew nothing. She

---

93. See *Man in History*, 73-75; *Glory of the Lord VII*, 475-476, 484.
94. Cf. Antonio Sicari, "La vita trinitaria e la preghiera," in Hans Urs von Balthasar et al (eds.), *Missione Ecclesiale*, 63-76. See also von Balthasar's introduction to Adrienne von Speyr's work, *Die Welt des Gebetes* (Einsiedeln: Johannes Verlag, 1951), 5ff.
95. "Maria in der kirchlichen Lehre," 58; *Explorations II: Spouse of the Word*, 177; *Mary for Today*, 70-72.
96. *Elucidations*, 96.

wants others to share in her grace. Accordingly, she "makes some part of her immaculateness flow out over the bride, the Church."[97] And indeed the Church continues in some sense to be "re-virginized."[98]

The image of the mantle appeals to von Balthasar also because it expresses how the Church is not a cosmos closed in on itself. As instrument and sacrament of Christ's salvation in and for the world, the Church is to communicate Christ in a maternal manner to the whole of humanity. Love, the highest of charisms, is the sheltering atmosphere that embraces all (1 Cor 16:14).[99]

Giving Birth to the Logos — Giving Birth to Heaven

Entering further into the dimensions of Marian maternity in the Church, von Balthasar wants to open us to a discovery that still has to be sufficiently appreciated, namely, the Marian principle and our Christian life as a creaturely participation in the trinitarian processions.[100]

In the incarnation and paschal mystery, the Logos has descended and been "born" among us within history and in the midst of our cosmos. The fruit of this "event" has been our creaturely participation in the trinitarian processions of love. In Pauline language, *in the Spirit* we are *in Christ* and, as such, we have been made "sons in the Son" of the Father. This begins hiddenly on earth and reaches fullness, openly, in heaven. From the early Church Fathers to the various mystical strands of thought throughout the centuries, it has always been realized that we are not just baptized into this reality, but continually being "fashioned" in the Spirit of the Logos. In other words, our Christian faith journey is characterized by a trinitarian dynamism in which we grow daily.

---

97. *Explorations II: Spouse of the Word*, 177.
98. *Theo-Drama III*, 334.
99. See *Explorations IV: Spirit and Institution*, 156.
100. *Theo-Drama V*, 462ff; *Theo-Drama II*, 302ff.

While Medieval mystics emphasized the individual dimension of the indwelling of the Trinity, von Balthasar proposes
that we rediscover the ecclesial-social aspect of the trinitarian
dynamism of Christian faith. It is in this context that he
underlines the Marian maternal principle of the Church.
Citing Hugo Rahner, he refers us to Cyril of Alexandria's dogmatics, who links the ever new "event" of Christ being formed
in us with Christ's birth from Mary:

> For Cyril too the pattern of this divine birth in the
> heart of the believer, a birth that is continually being
> repeated, is the unique incarnation of the Logos from
> the Holy Virgin. Thus our sanctification is a continual
> copying, in Christ's mystical body, of Christ's birth
> from Mary.[101]

Unlike Medieval and Spanish mystics, who left out the
theme of the Church and her archetype Mary in their treatment of creaturely participation in the innertrinitarian
process, von Balthasar believes our era is one of discovering
the theme of giving birth to Christ from the heart of the
Church/Mary.

He looks to the Fathers for hints on how to proceed in our
thinking this through. He notes, for instance, that under the
influence of Irenaeus, who sees the Word of God as allowing
himself to be "carried" by humankind and humankind as
"making room" for the Word, Hippolytus arrives at a position
where he says that the Logos is being born constantly out of
the heart of the Church and, through her, in and out of the
hearts of believers.[102] In the Letter to Diognetus he reads that
the Logos, who proceeds from the Father and "seemed to be
new and yet was found to be old, is constantly being born anew
in the hearts of the saints."[103] Origen teaches that the soul
becomes the "woman who is with child" and "has received the

---

101. *Theo-Drama V*, 467. Cf. Hugo Rahner, "Die Gottgeburt: Die Lehre der Kirchenväter von
   der Geburt Christi in den Herzen der Gläubigen," in *Zeitschrift für Katholische Theologie* 59
   (1935), 333-418.
102. *Antichr.* 61.
103. Letter to Diognetus, 11, 2, commenting on Hippolytus, *In Comm. Daniel* 1, 10, 8.

seed of the Word of God."[104] The whole Church "being with child" produces the mystical body of Christ in the multiplicity of her members.

Both in imitation of and participation in Christ's birth from Mary, von Balthasar reflects on how the Word, "born" in the heart of the Father, is implanted through baptism in the hearts of believers, who then, through the Spirit and the Church/Mary's maternity, are shaped by the Spirit of the Logos.

It is in this vein that he writes of the Church's Marian mission as one of giving "birth to heaven" through the birth of the Word, the Logos in us and among us. The Word allows himself to take shape in the totality of his body-bride and in her individual members (the believers). It is in involvement in this ever new "event" that we find ourselves participating in a lively manner in the ever new mystery of Christmas.[105]

If sanctification in the mystical body of Christ is, as Cyril of Alexandria points out, a continuous imitation of the birth of Christ from Mary, this should not, however, be limited to a merely ethical imitation. And this, von Balthasar contends, is what in our own age we have begun to understand more deeply. We are beginning to glimpse something of our participation in Mary's generation of the Logos. In other words, we are beginning to see how we share in the inner-trinitarian processions as they have been made known to us in the economy of salvation.

In his Word and his Spirit, God has given himself completely to what is other than himself, namely, creation. As a human creature made mother of God, Mary's role in the Church is intimately associated with the radical movement of love between God and creation. As the one in whom the Word became flesh, and in whom the Word become eucharist was placed anew in maternal care, and upon whom the Spirit descended anew at Pentecost, Mary-become-the-Church

---

104. Origen, *In Ex.* 10, 3.
105. *Theo-Drama III,* 353.

mediates trinitarian grace. It was this that was lacking in Medieval mysticism:

> Thus concludes our survey of the Church's mystical tradition with regard to the creature's participation in the internal "processions" of the Trinity. We enter on this participation, of course, through the *oikonomia*, the birth of the Logos in human nature; but this birth remains abstract and unintelligible unless we take account of the two factors that make it possible, namely, the Father's sending of the overshadowing Holy Spirit and humankind's consent in the womb of the Holy Virgin. The latter's theological relevance almost entirely disappeared from view in medieval mysticism, even though in Tauler (and still more in Suso) it remained an object of personal devotion.[106]

But we are only beginning to discover the implications of the link between the doctrine of Mary as mother of God and the mystery of the Church:

> The ultimate reason for this is that even in the Fathers — apart from the few exceptions such as Irenaeus — it was seen too exclusively as the physical (or ethical) model for the Church's mysteriological activity. Only in more recent times was it realized that Mary is a mediatrix of the graces of the Trinity: she mediates in and with the Church (since she is Mother of God) and together with her Son and as the model of the Church. We need to reflect further, however, on the mediatorial character of Mary/Ecclesia even in eternal life: there . . . the earthly missions are not suspended but, rather, brought to perfection.[107]

---

106. *Theo-Drama V,* 467.
107. *Theo-Drama V,* 467-468.

Mary, Memory of the Church

Taking his lead from John Paul II, one of the ways von Balthasar writes of the prophetic dimension of the Marian principle is to refer to Mary as the "memory of the Church."[108] Mary's motherly preservation of Jesus' words and deeds is recorded in the gospels (cf. Lk 2:19, 52). Her whole life was a formation in each mystery being communicated throughout the life of her Son, Jesus Christ. Nobody else has a similarly unbroken memory from the first moment of incarnation to the cross.[109]

Her progressive penetration of the gospel depths reached its fruition when, with her assumption into heaven, she finally came to know the entire depth and breadth of God's plans and her place in his plan of salvation. This knowledge of the heart and mind has now become a "treasure chest" to be handed out among the faithful under her mantle. As the Seat of Wisdom and Church-teacher, she is now active from heaven teaching us.

> When Mary receives the angel's announcement that the Spirit will overshadow her and she will bear a child, "her experience inundates her knowledge, with the result that she receives more insight, and at the same time everything becomes more mysterious than she thought. The mystery grows in her: it becomes brighter and yet accumulates into a store of knowledge that is undisclosed, a treasure from which all generations of the Church will draw sustenance in order to penetrate into her mystery. They will never come to an end."[110]

---

108. For this section, see especially *Mary for Today*, 33-45. Cf. John Paul II, "Calendis Ianuariis" (Homily preached in St. Peter's on 1 January 1987), AAS 79 (1987), 1146-1150.
109. *Mary for Today*, 37.
110. *Theo-Drama V*, 496. Von Balthasar is quoting from Adrienne von Speyr, *Das Word und die Mystik, Bd. II: Objektive Mystik* (Einsiedeln: Johannes Verlag, 1980), 26-27.

From the very beginning, Mary was active in communicating this mystery. Starting with the fact that Mary lived in
John's household, von Balthasar comments that it would be
surprising if she did not relate to John many of the words she
had stored in her heart, especially those concerning the gospel
of love of the trinitarian God.[111] Accordingly, he believes that
many new insights into revelation gained within the life of the
Church over the centuries are to be linked to the maternal-
prophetic dimension of the Marian principle.

This is also confirmed for him through an account, to which
he refers often, of a vision which Gregory Thaumaturgus had
as he prepared for his ordination as bishop. It is recounted by
Gregory of Nyssa, and it is the first Marian apparition found in
trustworthy sources.[112] The fruit of this apparition was a
credal formula that von Balthasar considers to be one of the
finest and clearest credal formulae we have. In the apparition,
at Mary's word John introduces Gregory in clear language into
the mystery of the Trinity.

Throughout the centuries, Mary's memory is as fresh as the
first day. She is now the teacher of the Church. Von Balthasar
believes it would be impossible to write a history of Mary's
teaching through the centuries. It will only be in heaven that
we shall see how much the Church owes to Mary in understanding the faith.

Once again, von Balthasar does not intend merely a devotional perspective. He sees this aspect of Mary's maternity
expressed in the contribution of the charismatic/Marian
dimension of the Church. During the forty days between his
resurrection and ascension, Jesus gave the apostles understanding of scripture combined with theological and pastoral
knowledge. But this was placed within the deeper spiritual
womb of womanly contemplation. Arising from this consideration, it can be said that the Marian principle communicates

---

111. *Mary for Today,* 41.
112. See *Mary for Today,* 41-52; "Our Lady in Monasticism," 53; *Office of Peter,* 225. Cf. PG
    10:984-988; 46:912-913.

Christian wisdom in a maternal fashion to the apostolic Church.[113] Von Balthasar goes so far as to say:

> The gospels are the fruit of contemplation, brought forth from the womb of the primitive Church, and for this reason, they cannot give us any other image of the Trinity than the Marian one, that is to say, embodied in the actual life of these persons depicted in revelation, principally of the incarnate God himself, and explicable only in that context.[114]

Citing Adrienne von Speyr, von Balthasar comments that "because Mary was so contemplative on earth she can be so active in heaven, namely by letting the Church share in the superabundance of her memory."[115]

Mary in the Church as Cosmic Mother

The gospel message is cosmic in its dimensions. And cosmic is the vision that we find in one of von Balthasar's early works, *Heart of the World,* written in the light of Adrienne von Speyr's mystical intuitions.[116] His treatment of the theme of the maturation of the world through history reflects thought running from Irenaeus to Teilhard de Chardin. Cosmic progress can never be reduced to technological advancement. The Church is the "structure" of the triune God that brings creation to completion.[117]

The law of cosmic progress is primarily the law of personal progress in our relationship with the Lord of history (2 Cor 3:18).[118] As an intensified period of this progress, the time of the Church involves the working out of the presence of Christ

---

113. *Explorations II: Spouse of the Word,* 177.
114. *Explorations I: The Word Made Flesh,* 197-198.
115. *Mary for Today,* 43.
116. Cf. *Mein Werk,* 85.
117. *Credo: Meditations on the Apostles' Creed* (Edinburgh: T&T Clark, 1990), 84.
118. *Man in History,* 136ff. See Joseph Ratzinger, *Volk und Haus Gottes in Augustins Lehre von der Kirche* (Munich, 1954), 197-218.

in both the mystical body of the Church and in world history.[119] The whole cosmos' unconscious expectation is included in humankind's great yearning and hope: to attain the freedom of the "Sonship" of God (cf. Rom 8:19-22) and to participate, in Jesus Christ, in the "firstfruits of the Spirit" that lie beyond humankind (Rom 8:23) in the bosom of the Father.

In his writings, von Balthasar contends that the Marian principle of the Church has to do with the cosmic widening of Christ's heart drawing all people and things to himself and, in him, to the Father. Mary has become in all of us the cosmic Mother. In the lyrical style of *Heart of the World,* von Balthasar composes the following as words addressed by Jesus to all of us, the Church:

> You have sprung forth from my heart and I have rested under your heart. You, to whom I gave birth with much suffering at the cross, will be prostrate in painful labor with me until the end of the world. Your image mysteriously blurs to merge with the image of my virginal Mother. She is an individual woman, but in you she becomes the cosmic Mother. For in you my individual heart, too, widens to become the heart of the world. You yourself are the holy heart of the nations, holy because of me, but unifying the world for me, making my blood circulate throughout the body of history. In you my redemption ripens, I myself grow to my full stature, until I, two-in-one with you, and in the bond of the two-in-one flesh — you, my Bride and my Body — will place at the feet of the Father the Kingdom which we are. The bond of our love is the meaning of the world. In it all things reach fulfillment. For the meaning of the world is love.[120]

The meaning of the world is love. It is Mary-Church who draws the world toward her "magnetic center," namely,

---

119. *Man in History,* 173.
120. *Heart of the World,* 202.

Christical.[121] There is more than an echo in von Balthasar's theology of the Eastern understanding of the Church as the definitive incarnation of the divine *Sophia,* gathering together in her bosom all the seeds of the Logos, scattered throughout creation and the history of salvation.[122] The Church's essence is the unity already reached and yet also in formation. For von Balthasar, the Mother of God, the Church as mother, and cosmic unity are directly linked.

The Marian Form of Paradise

In his much-loved metaphorical mode of expression, von Balthasar alludes to the ultimate form of the world as the child-world, and speaks of the Christ-embracing cosmos as a suckling infant dreaming in the arms of the Virgin Mary.[123] For him this image conveys a theology of history in its fulfillment.

Not only is the Marian yes relevant for the earthly economy but, as the eschatological nuptial image of the Spirit and the Bride (Rv 21) indicates, it continues in eternal life. Mary's universal missionary ray, which extends to the entire humanity, will extend right into eternity. For von Balthasar, this is the logic of the data of revelation:

> If even the missions of the twelve tribes of Israel and the twelve apostles of the Lamb are to remain forever in the heavenly Jerusalem (Rv 21:12, 14), how much more will the mission of Mary remain in this Jerusalem, since she is the holy bride and spouse of the Lamb, and the one who, through her consent, gave the world its Savior.[124]

---

121. *Man in History,* 173.
122. See "How weighty is the argument from 'uninterrupted tradition' to justify the male priesthood?" *Communio* 23 (1996), 185-192, espec., 189-190.
123. *Heart of the World,* 211.
124. *Theo-Drama V,* 468.

Mary is our "door" to heaven and this far more than Peter, who is simply the door-keeper; she is the help we need so that our birth into heaven may be successful.[125] But there is also something more. In considering what the final form of our sharing in the life of paradise will be like, echoing Dante, von Balthasar writes that it will be Marian. Not only is Mary the definitive "teleotype" of the New Testament Church. Our ultimate fulfillment will be our Marian sharing in the end-sacrament of "the whole triune God revealed in the world of transfigured creation."[126]

The final *visio beatifica* will be no individualistic, static or narrow achievement.[127] God is not an object but a life that is going on eternally and yet is ever new. The doctrine of the assumption indicates that our final destiny is to live, not over against God, but in him. Paradise is participation in the "event" that is from all eternity the divine dialogue. Accordingly, the ultimate scene that has already begun in Christ is described in the Book of Revelation as a nuptial dialogue: the Lord says, "I am coming soon" (Rv 22:7) and the Spirit and the Bride respond, "Come" (Rv 22:17. 20). In this dialogue of love, our knowing God will be "at once a beholding and a journeying."

Our final homecoming in paradise will be the reciprocity of love that is found in the Godhead itself between the divine Persons. In this regard, at the conclusion of the second section of his trilogy, *Theo-Drama,* von Balthasar remarks:

> What does God gain from the world? An additional gift, given to the Son by the Father, but equally a gift made by the Son to the Father, and by the Spirit to both. It is a gift because, through the distinct operations of each of the three Persons, the world acquires an inward share in the divine exchange of life; as a result the world is able to take the divine things it has

---

125. *Mary for Today,* 30.
126. *New Elucidations,* 103; *Glory of the Lord III,* 82; *Theo-Drama III,* 338. Cf. Dante's *Paradise* 31.
127. See *Theo-Drama V,* 425ff.

received from God, together with the gift of being created, and return them to God as a divine *gift*.[128]

Christ wants to be in us to stand before the Father, and it is
in us that he wants us to be in the Father. The *visio beatifica* will
be for us, therefore, a participation in the living "event" of God
himself. That is where the Marian principle extends right into
paradise. God's plan for Mary was so vast as to create her
mother of God and mother of the Church. It is within the
Marian "transparency" to Christ that the Church will participate in the circulation of life and love that is paradise where
God is all in all. Hence the titles attributed to Mary such as
"Mary, Queen of Heaven" and "Queen of the Angels" and
"Queen of all the Saints."[129]

While all of this is the eschatological end point toward
which we are striving, it is always necessary to recall that
already now we live in the "memory of the future." The
Marian principle is always operative in the Church opening up
paradise for us:

> If paradise is being in God, and if the triune God is an
> endless exchange among the persons of God the
> Father, God the Son and God the Holy Spirit, then
> God will draw his perfected creation into this flow of
> divine life. At that time, as the Lord of the Apocalypse
> says, each one shall receive a new name. . . . Each one
> will finally know who he or she is in reality, and conse-
> quently each person will at this time be able to make of
> themselves a fully authentic and unique gift. And this
> self-giving will be common to all, so that we will not
> only plunge eternally into God's ever newer depths,
> but also into the inexhaustible depths of our fellow
> creatures, both angels and humans. . . . For all eternity
> God will remain a mystery, and we will not ever ex-
> haust the full depth of the grace whereby each of us is
> permitted to participate in this mystery by the very

128. *Theo-Drama V*, 475-476.
129. *Threefold Garland*, 133-139.

fact that we *are* and that we can love one another. . . . The prayer of Mary . . . when uttered in eternal life is an expression of the blessed cycle whereby God is always greeting us anew as his children and we are endlessly sending up to him a grateful song of praise.[130]

Conclusion

The last three chapters have attempted to say something about how Mary continues to live in the Church. It is a significant presence. So much so that, in the light of von Balthasar's writings, Klaus Hemmerle re-reads the features of the Church (*notae ecclesiae* — one, holy, catholic and apostolic) and comments that there is a fifth constitutive feature, namely, that as well as being one, holy, catholic and apostolic, the Church is Marian.[131]

At the conclusion of part 3, we saw how Mary's faith experience revolves around being virgin, bride, and mother. Part 4 has been an attempt to trace how this archetypal faith experience flows into the Church. What we have attempted to show is that there is a Marian transparency with three distinctive features — virginal openness to God's mystery, bridal response to the Word's self-emptying that creates communion, and maternal missionary activity linked to the Holy Spirit.

By way of a final summary, it is helpful to present von Balthasar's notion of three "circles" of the Church.[132] Reminiscent of the apocalyptic version of the three rings in the Church, and analogous to circular waves spreading out and lapping over each other reciprocally when a stone is thrown into water, von Balthasar proposes an image of the Church marked by concentric circles. Just as the biggest stone thrown

130. *Threefold Garland*, 138-139.
131. See Klaus Hemmerle, "Das Neue ist älter: Hans Urs von Balthasar und die Orientierung der Theologie" *Erbe und Auftrag* (Beuron) 57 (1981), 81-98, espec. 91-95.
132. See *Explorations II: Spouse of the Word*, 315-331; "Prägung der Kirche," 263-279. Cf. William Link, *Gestalt und Gestaltlosigkeit der Kirche* (Rome: P.U.G., 1970), 232-353.

into water provokes a ripple that spreads and surrounds the others, so too among the circles of the Church there is one that circles all others — the Marian circle. The ray of her mission contains all the others because she is co-extensive with the Church.

Von Balthasar is encouraged in proposing this image of circles within the Church's unity by what he discovers of the dynamic understanding of the Church reality right up to the Enlightenment. For instance, John of Pecham proposed a multi-layered unity of the Church in terms of love and holiness into which unity of obedience to the hierarchy was intergrated:

> For him, Church unity is (1) unity of love, by which all are one heart and one soul; (2) unity of divinization (that is, of grace), which makes all members of the one Christ; (3) unity of ecclesiastical communion in faith and the sacraments; (4) unity of the hierarchical connection, to which belong the common obedience and also the unity of the apostolic succession from Christ; and (5) unity of common sentiments (unanimity).[133]

In the light also of Vatican II's milestone decision to insert the chapter on Mary into the constitution on the Church, von Balthasar outlines three circles of the Church's unity as follows.

Firstly, he writes of the inner circle of the Church. It is the "supra-ministerial" Marian dimension of the Church. Because the first cell of the Church is the Christ-Mary relationship, the inner Marian circle is the all-embracing holiness that unites us within the spousal encounter with Jesus Christ. The inner Marian circle is the Church of the saints, where the mystery of the triune life is perfectly received, embodied, lived in communion and communicated.

---

133. *Explorations II: Spouse of the Word,* 178.

The second circle is the Petrine, ministerial or institutional one. It too is co-extensive with the Marian in its reach. The hierarchical, institutional dimension of the Church, itself vivified by the Holy Spirit, plays a formative, nourishing role within the Bride, ensuring contact with the transcendent form-giving source of the Christ event. It is through the eucharist, for example, that we "no longer live, but Christ lives in us" and we find ourselves in the bosom of the Father.

Finally, the third circle is the fruit of the inter-action of the Marian and Petrine principles, namely, existential Marian transparency of the whole life of the Church radiating Christ to the world. It is the feminine Marian profile of the whole Church. As a sphere of the life of the gospel lived in holiness, the whole Church sees in Mary what she is and what she is called to become. The people of God has a Marian profile. And this is the Church's beauty. In a certain sense, it is by re-living Mary that the Church rediscovers what she is and how she is to be: servant of the Father, Spouse of the Word, vessel of the Spirit and as such mother of all.

Part 5

Signs of the Marian Principle Today

In his encyclical letter on the dignity of woman, *Mulieris Dignitatem,* John Paul II cites von Balthasar in saying that Mary is "Queen of the Apostles" without claiming apostolic powers for herself. She possesses something else and something more.[1] This book has attempted to open up aspects of this "something more." It would be incomplete, however, if it did not include a chapter on some of the concrete signs of the visibility of the Marian principle in the Church.

On the one hand, von Balthasar writes that after the death and resurrection of Jesus, Mary disappeared into the heart of the Church to remain there as a real presence that always gives place to her Son. To experience the reality of this presence, he points us in particular to the Eastern Church, the life of which is permeated and perfumed by a living Marian principle.[2]

But in the course of his writings, talks and interviews, von Balthasar also points to concrete signs of the Marian principle and comments on their relevancy in the contemporary situation of the Church.[3] In the following short chapters, we shall present some of the observations he makes in each case.

---

1. *Mulieris Dignitatem* (15 August 1988), 27, fn. 55: AAS 80 (1988) II, 1653-1729, espec. 1718, quoting from *New Elucidations,* 196.
2. *Office of Peter,* 159.
3. See, for instance, *La Realtà e la Gloria.*

The Marian Principle and Renewal
in the Church

Henri de Lubac has remarked that there is a positive relationship between von Balthasar's ecclesiology and that of the Second Vatican Council.[4] There is a coincidence of themes and a parallel goal. Von Balthasar himself observed that the abiding concern throughout his work and writings, namely, that the true face of the Church's catholicity should radiate in the world today, was at the heart of what the Second Vatican Council wanted to achieve.[5]

Prior to the Council, he wrote that a new *sentire Ecclesiae,* a feeling of being Church, was emerging, and it was Marian.[6] The Council's spiritual "watershed," as it has been called — the insertion of the chapter on Mary into its constitution on the Church — confirmed his intuition. And it is perhaps particularly von Balthasar's underlining of the Marian principle in the Church that is his greatest contribution to contemporary post-Conciliar ecclesiology. Throughout his writings he keeps his eye on the themes of the opening and closing chapters of *Lumen Gentium,* namely, the mystery of the Church and her Marian nature. And this is important for renewal:

> Perhaps it is particularly necessary for our times to look at Mary. To see her as she shows herself, not as we like to imagine her. To see her, above all, in order not to forget her essential role in the work of salvation and in the Church. She really shows herself and defines herself as the archetypal Church, upon whose form we

4. *Paradoxe et Mystère* (Paris: Editions Montaigne, 1967), 181. See also Fessio, *The Origin of the Church,* 258ff.
5. *Test Everything,* 17ff.
6. *Razing the Bastions,* 93ff. In an interview in 1985, von Balthasar reaffirmed the contents of this book inspired by de Lubac. See *Test Everything,* 13.

should form ourselves. We: that means every single Christian and it means, perhaps even more, our image of what the Church is. We are for ever concerned with reshaping and improving the Church in accordance with the demands of the time, following the criticisms of opponents and our own models. But do we not thereby lose sight of the one fulfilled standard, indeed the Model? Should we not constantly keep our eyes fixed on Mary in our reforms, not in any way to multiply the Marian feastdays, devotions or indeed definitions, but rather simply to know what Church, what ecclesial Spirit, and what ecclesial behavior really is?[7]

As these words show, it is not that von Balthasar is recommending more devotions or definitions. At the dawn of the third millennium, he invites us, rather, to a deeper recognition of the Marian principle in all its dimensions within the very life and mystery of the Church. The objective Petrine holiness of the Church is, of course, a vital aspect of the mystical body, but it is not the whole Church. The Marian dimension needs to be discovered, because it is only in her Marian essence that the Church is comprehensible in all her hierarchical offices and functions.[8]

There is an urgency in his writing on this theme. In a "male functionalist world," he comments, there is a risk that to a large extent we have become a Church of permanent discussions, organizations, advisory committees, congresses, synods, commissions, academies, parties, pressure-groups, functions, structures and restructuring, sociological experiments, statistics, that is, more than ever a "male Church" lacking the

---

7. See "Maria in der kirchlichen Lehre," 78.
8. *Explorations I: The Word Made Flesh*, 201. See also Leo Scheffczyk, *Katholische Glaubenswelt: Wahrheit und Gestalt* (Aschaffenburg: Paul Pattloch Verlag, 1978), 289-291; *La Chiesa: Aspetti della Crisi Postconciliare e corretta interpretazione del Vaticano II* (Milan: Jaca Book, 1998), 103-112; and Hanspeter Heinz, "Variationen zum Thema 'Trinitarische Einheit': Theologische Aufbrüche im 20. Jahrhundert," in M. Böhnke and H. Heinz (eds.), *Im Gespräch mit dem dreieinen Gott: Elemente einer trinitarischen Theologie* (Düsseldorf: Patmos, 1985), 334-347; Rosemary Ruether, "New Thinking on the Church," *Cross Currents* 13 (1968), 110-113, espec. 111.

Marian "soul." Von Balthasar does not mince his words when describing the outcome:

> Without Mariology, Christianity threatens impercep- tibly to become inhuman. The Church becomes functionalistic, soulless, a hectic enterprise without any point of rest, made unfamiliar by the planners. And because, in this manly-masculine world, all that we have is one ideology replacing another, everything becomes polemical, critical, bitter, humorless, and ultimately boring, and people in their masses run away from such a Church.[9]

---

9. *Elucidations,* 112.

A Spirituality for Everyone

There is a growing appreciation today that renewal in the Church and authentic spirituality are linked. The large 1997 ecumenical gathering in Graz, Austria, has pointed in this direction as did John Paul II's letter in preparation for the celebration of the jubilee 2000, *Tertio Millennio Adveniente*. The issue of spirituality is central in von Balthasar's writings. W. Link has gone so far as to suggest that he is ultimately concerned not so much with sketching a systematic ecclesiology as with promoting a Church spirituality.[10]

He views the "spirituality of spiritualities" in the Church as Marian.[11] As we have just seen, he is not referring to a particular set of prayers or devotions but rather to something broader. Christian spirituality is a way of life which, von Balthasar observes, almost by definition, is a Marian spirituality.[12] Why? Because the vocation of each Christian and of the Church in her totality is, as it were, to "live" Mary in her transparency to Christ, to the point where it can be said: "It is no longer I who live but Christ who lives in me" (Gal 2:20). The Marian spirituality has to do with letting Christ be formed in us through the work of the Spirit.

Mary's own spirituality centers on a transparent yes to God. This is what is common to everyone in the Church prior to all differentiations into more specific spiritualities. There are three basic dimensions involved:

Virginal openness to the mystery of God's love and the "indifference" of being available for whatever God wants. This is the fundamental point of Christian spirituality — knowing and

---

10. See *Gestalt und Gestaltlosigkeit der Kirche*, 427.
11. See "The Gospel as Norm and Critique of all Spirituality in the Church," *Explorations III: Creator Spirit*, 295 and "Spirituality" in *Explorations I: The Word Made Flesh*, 211ff.
12. See *Explorations I: The Word Made Flesh*, 211ff.

believing that God has chosen and loved us and that we can chose him in response. It is our yes to God, given day by day. The Church Fathers spoke of this in terms of "impassibility" (*apatheia*), the Medieval world spoke of it as "imperturbability" (not depending on things of the world), while Ignatius of Loyola spoke of "indifference," that being happy with everything as God has arranged it for us.

Bridal response to the Word. The increased attention to the Word of God in recent times is, in von Balthasar's opinion, the most welcome and undoubtedly the most hopeful sign in the Catholic world today.[13] Mary's spirituality is centered on the Word becoming flesh, becoming eucharist, becoming Church. In our lives, living this spirituality means putting the Word of God into practice right to the point of participating in our daily lives in Christ's kenosis on the cross, and in this way building up the Church's communion.

Maternal "Christophorous existence."[14] Mary is the *Theotokos*. She bears God, and her life can be described as a "Christophorous existence." As well as being chosen to allow Christ to be generated within us, every baptized person is called to carry Christ to others, to the world. Living this "Christophorous existence" involves key elements of Mary's spirituality — love of neighbor, mutual love, listening to the Holy Spirit, the eucharist, and love of the Church.[15]

Mary's life was built up as prayer and fruitful contemplation. Looking at her, we discover that contemplation is not an individualistic affair but eminently social, because its fruits flow into the life of the Church. It is the fly-wheel of contemplation that keeps the Church active; it is her inner spring that gives unconditional fruitfulness to all her external actions. This contemplation in the Church is not split from action. Our "orthopraxy" and "ortho-doxy," as von Balthasar writes,

---

13. *Who is a Christian?* 29-32; *Prayer* 29ff.
14. *Glory of the Lord I,* 562; *Explorations IV: Spirit and Institution,* 453; "Maria nel Nostro Tempo," 68.
15. Cf. "Life and Institution," *Communio* 12 (1985), 25-32; *Razing the Bastions,* 73ff; *Explorations IV: Spirit and Institution,* 204ff; 224ff, 341ff.

constantly requires the presence of "ortho-agápe" (Rv 2:4-5) grounded in this Marian contemplation.[16] But he sees an expression of all of this in the monasteries of contemplatives in the Church, the Church's official prayer and the new forms of contemplatives in the world.

---

16. *You Have Words of Eternal Life,* 260.

Holiness, the Saints, Founders and Charisms

Von Balthasar once wrote that "bombs" may fall on the Church from all kinds of external difficulties, and these may indeed prompt change, but ultimately it is the explosive energies of holiness that count.[17] The Marian principle is manifest in myriad forms of holiness that render the Church a *living* Christian community.

All the saints, and this includes the everyday saints, are held in high regard by von Balthasar. Not that he admires pious hagiographies. To the contrary, he urges us to read the theological significance of the saints as a continuing of Mary's role in the formation of the Church. In an expression adopted from Adrienne von Speyr, he writes of them as "Mary's train" in that their radiance comes from the innermost center of the Marian-ecclesial consent to the word of God.[18]

Although, in general, the saints' great efficacy is posthumous, while alive they are "regenerative energies in the Church."[19] In the midst of the crowd things begin to change around them — hearts and structures change. He points to Alexander Solzhenitsyn's example of Matryona. Something extraordinary radiated from this ordinary person. Solzhenitsyn's own comment at the end of his short story captures this: "None of us who lived close to her perceived that she was that one righteous person without whom, as the saying goes, the village could not endure. . . . Nor the city. . . . Nor all our land."[20]

The saints establish and radiate the Church as *communio,* and as such their holiness breaks through the prejudices that

---

17. *Razing the Bastions,* 23ff.
18. See *First Glance at Adrienne von Speyr,* 72ff.
19. *Theo-Drama IV,* 466, 442ff.
20. See *Matryona's Home and Other Stories* (Harmondsworth: Penguin, 1983), 47, cited in *Elucidations,* 100.

people continually erect around the institutional aspect of the Church because it shows the transcendental significance of this aspect. Their holiness appeals irresistible to sincere inquirers: "If only all of you were like these," is what the world says.[21] The saints, in von Balthasar's view, are living commentaries on scripture and canonical forms for Church life. They are the living tradition, and in them the Church magisterium's infallibility is mirrored not so much in concepts as in a lived infallibility of holiness.[22]

On a more concrete pastoral level, von Balthasar is well aware that there are many aspects of the Church that no longer speak to people today. Many, especially the young, say yes to Christ but no to the Church. Here, the importance of models arises. Not just models of saints of the past, but models of holiness lived out in the present. He sees proof of this in young people today who, through the example of contemporary models, see and understand not that the Church is powerful but that she is receptive.[23]

A second issue is that of changes in the Church's structures. He clearly re-affirms the structural continuity of the Church linked to ordained ministry and sacraments. He knows that mere changes in structures are not the solution to issues facing the Church today. Yet, he is also conscious that "precisely because the Church's structure is given from above, something mysterious and not merely human contrivance, it can, while retaining its basic form, be susceptible of modifications, the outcome of a living dialogue between the various states, one in which the whole Church is concerned. In this, new forms may make their appearance, which . . . have a fresh, distinctive stamp, and are truly the work of the Holy Spirit."[24]

Apart from regenerative energy which comes from the lives of the saints, von Balthasar also has in mind the prophetic

---

21. *Explorations I: The Word Made Flesh*, 200.
22. *Razing the Bastions*, 86.
23. See Klaus Hemmerle and Hans Urs von Balthasar, "Institution: geflohen und gesucht," 137. See also *Test Everything*, 66.
24. *Explorations I: The Word Made Flesh*, 222.

dimensions of *charisms* that open up new collective experiences within the Church. These charisms are endowed by the third divine Person, who knows in each new era of history how to respond to its challenges by raising up new forms of discipleship for the upbuilding of the Church. Throughout Church history, in fact, there have always been saints with particular charisms or missions, who have caused holiness to spread like ripples in a pool, giving rise to new families in the Church. Examples such as Basil, Augustine, Benedict, Francis and Clare of Assisi, Catherine of Siena, Ignatius, Teresa of Avila, John of the Cross and, more recently, among others, Charles de Foucauld are mentioned by von Balthasar.[25]

The great founders of Orders and others who have special missions from God proceed "like lightning from heaven and light up some unique point of God's will for the Church." The "Church must receive them and herself embody their message." The saints with particular missions manifest "a new type of conformity to Christ inspired by the Holy Spirit and therefore a new illustration of how the gospel is to be lived . . . a new interpretation of revelation." Von Balthasar comments that while the hierarchy interprets the scriptural revelation of Christ, "we should not forget that this prompting [by the Spirit] is equally urgent in the saints, who are the 'living gospel.'"[26] Those with particular missions open new doors to the heart of revelation for today.

Von Balthasar links these charisms with Mary, because the Holy Spirit overshadowed her at the annunciation and again at Pentecost. He writes of the fundamental charism (*Grundcharisma*) in the Church, realized in Mary. In a way, he sees her as full of charisms. The Marian charism is the fundamental charism providing the true and universal spirit at the basis of all the various charisms in the Church.[27]

All of this leads von Balthasar to comment that if we want to look for a dawn in the difficulties of today, then we need to

---

25. See *Die Grossen Ordensregeln*.
26. *Two Sisters in the Spirit* (San Francisco: Ignatius Press, 1992), 23ff.
27. *Explorations III: Creator Spirit*, 295ff.

look to where Christianity appears not as a laboriously repeated doctrine but rather as a "breathtaking adventure."[28] Wherever genuine renewal is taking place in today's Church, the movement can be traced back to an outpouring from a prophetical, charismatic or mystical source.[29]

---

28. *Short Primer*, 17.
29. *Die Wahrheit ist symphonisch*, 91.

Mysticism and Theology

Let us now turn specifically to the theme of mysticism. By the "charism" of mysticism von Balthasar is not referring to a vague psychological phenomenon. Within the history of Western mysticism, Christian mysticism has a specific meaning with its supreme problem of union between the essentially one and what is essentially multiple. Von Balthasar refers us to the experience of many women mystics within the Christian tradition such as Hildegaard of Bingen (1098–1179), Julian of Norwich (fifteenth century), Mathilde of Hackeborn (born 1241), Mathilde of Magdeburg (1210–1285) and, of course, Adrienne von Speyr.

In his writings, he presents mysticism as that prophetic moment in the life of the Church in which an individual is endowed with a particular insight into the gospel. This mystical insight is intended for the whole Church and to be lived with a Marian *anima ecclesiastica*.[30] There is a double moment in mysticism. Firstly, that of the solitude of being "thrust" into the very bosom of God, the cataract of graces. The second is that of being directed back toward the community, to be in communion with all so as to build up that communion through the novelty of the interpretation of revelation with which the mystic has been endowed. Von Balthasar sees this as an eminently Marian movement. Mysticism is an expression of Mary's continuing ecclesial receptivity as partner of the Word and image of the Church.[31]

This dimension of the Marian principle is highlighted by von Balthasar in terms of its potential contribution to theology on two levels. Firstly, the example of Mary herself. Mary

---

30. *First Glance at Adrienne von Speyr*, 51-56.
31. Cf. *Prayer*, 96-97.

shows the vital unity between theological knowledge and life, theology and sanctity.[32] The Church Fathers honored Mary with the title *Theologos,* and she personifies theology as a nuptial encounter with the Word in a movement of reception, response and novelty.

Like Scheeben, von Balthasar understands theology as a dialogue between bride and bridegroom.[33] In living the Marian yes, theology is an "event" of "metamorphosis" in which we participate in the Son's own vision and knowing in God. This is why theology at the desk cannot supersede what von Balthasar terms a "kneeling theology,"[34] that is, a theology at prayer, reflecting the unity of faith and knowledge and an attitude of objectivity allied with one of reverence and awe.

In terms of theology, there is, however, a second and very important feature of the Marian principle. Writing of Mary, von Balthasar comments that both theological/pastoral knowledge and understanding have been placed deep within the spiritual womb of womanly contemplation.[35] The lived holiness of the Church contains doctrinal implications. It is primarily on this basis that he laments the divorce between theology and holiness which has existed since the Middle Ages.

His regret comes from the fact that the mystics yield great doctrinal wealth that has not been adequately considered in the realm of school theology.[36] Private spiritualities have been made out of what really were important missions sent for the Church. Accordingly, new theological and doctrinal insights and contributions are to be and should be expected from the Marian side of the Church. These contributions are

---

32. See von Balthasar's classical article on the subject, "Theology and Holiness," in *Explorations I: The Word Made Flesh,* 181-209. See also Juda Konda, *Das Verhältnis von Theologie und Heiligkeit im Werk Hans Urs von Balthasar* (Würzburg: Echter-Verlag, 1991).

33. See *Glory of the Lord* I, 104ff; *Explorations I: The Word Made Flesh,* 203.

34. *Explorations I: The Word Made Flesh,* 206ff; Konda, *Das Verhältnis von Theologie und Heiligkeit,* 155-159; Antonio Sicari, "Hans Urs von Balthasar: Theology and Holiness," *Communio* 16 (1989), 351-365, espec. 363.

35. *Explorations II: Spouse of the Word,* 165.

36. See also Adrienne von Speyr's similar views in B. Albrecht, *Eine Theologie des Katholischen* II, 37-66.

characterized by a converging faith moving toward the unity of theology rather than its fragmentation.

Certainly, objective revelation was concluded with the death of the last apostle, but it does not follow, he writes, that in the Church of saints nothing further happens that touches on revelation. Indeed, he asks, if the miracles of absolution and consecration bring about an ever new presence of the events of Good Friday and Easter within the Church, why should it not be the same with the constant repetition of the theological existence of the Lord in the life of his faithful and saints?[37]

In this context, von Balthasar contends that more should and could be demanded of one of his favorite saints, Thérèse of Lisieux, than simply a pious account of her life.[38] That Thérèse has been named the thirty-third doctor of the Church is due in no small measure to his writings on this topic.

37. *Explorations I: The Word Made Flesh,* 204. See Achille Romani, *L'immagine della Chiesa,* 17ff; Konda, *Das Verhältnis von Theologie und Heiligkeit,* 139-145.
38. *Explorations I: The Word Made Flesh,* 192. See also *Two Sisters in the Spirit,* 28ff; "Die Hoffnung der kleinen Therese," in B. Albrecht/H. U. v. Balthasar, *Thérèse von Lisieux: Zum Gedenken ihres 100. Geburtstages am 2. Januar 1973* (Leutesdorf: Johannes Verlag, 1973), 23.

The Marian Principle and Women
in the Church

A sensibility to the feminine is a feature in von Balthasar's writings.[39] He considers the Marian principle visible particularly in women in the Church. It is in this light that he finds many things in the feminist demands comprehensible, and adds his voice to those who claim that the dignity of the vocation of women should be better recognized in the Church.[40] He holds out the hope that through her Marian principle, the Church will be an enlightening model for our society that forgets how much it owes to woman and her femininity.[41]

The Marian Authority

From von Balthasar's various writings that we have already examined emerges what might be called a Marian "authority" of love that is particularly found in women:

1) First and foremost, on the basis of what we have seen in previous chapters, he sees woman as the privileged bearer of the Church's essence as love and unity. The primary role of women in the ecclesial sphere is to guard the flame of those fundamental values of the Church as love, where service (and not servility!) has primacy.[42]

---

39. Susanne Greiner, "La dignità della donna," in K. Lehmann and W. Kasper, *Hans Urs von Balthasar: Figura e Opera* (Casale Monferratto: Piemme, 1991), 367-382, espec. 367. See also Ludmila Grygiel's article, "La Missione della donna negli scritti di Adrienne von Speyr," in *Hans Urs von Balthasar, Missione Ecclesiale*, 125-131.
40. *La Realtà e la Gloria*, 155.
41. See "Maria nel nostro tempo," 68-71. See also Piero Coda, "Teologia e antropologia nella 'Mulieris Dignitatem'" *Nuova Umanità* 11 (1989), n. 61, 9-29.
42. See *New Elucidations*, 187ff; "Church as 'Caritas'" in *Elucidations*, 245ff.

2) Woman is the privileged place where God is able and willing to be received into this world. Women often have a better understanding of total commitment and are in this sense nearer to the primary demand of radical discipleship of the gospel.[43]

3) Mary's role can be viewed as a model for an intensely responsible activity of women in the building up of Christ's body-bride under the prompting of the Spirit. A proper understanding of Mary and the Church also points to a deeper understanding of the role women play in the new evangelization.[44]

4) More than ever before, woman's role today comes into prominence in the context of the predominantly male-oriented technological civilization in which we live.[45] In a motherless and fatherless culture, von Balthasar points to woman as guardian of a sociality that provides a home in our technical desert. As the one who symbolizes security, home and shelter, she guards the meaning of being human. Von Balthasar also comments that it is to woman that we must look to get us out of an increasingly history-less world.

5) Echoing von Balthasar, Barbara Albrecht points to a feminine-Marian "Spirit-role" as a principle of unity within the Church and the world.[46] Von Balthasar's writings clearly indicate there is a link between Mary, woman and the Spirit in such a role in the Church.

6) Von Balthasar's reflections on the Marian principle in the Church can also be seen as a clarification of what it is to be man. Woman helps man reach full humanity by pointing to what is essential.[47] Men too will find their true identity in the Marian dimension of ecclesial existence.

---

43. *New Elucidations*, 203.
44. See "Maria in der kirchlichen Lehre," 66.
45. See *New Elucidations*, 187ff.
46. See "Is there an Objective Type 'Woman'?" in Helmut Moll, *The Church and Women: A Compendium* (San Francisco: Ignatius Press, 1988), 35-49, here 49.
47. "Maria nel nostro tempo," 70.

Some Representatives

Life and theology go together for von Balthasar. His theological vision of woman is no mere abstract speculation. He knew many significant women in the Church, and the reader will note the high profile given to women in his theological dialogue with various representatives of the Western intellecutal history (*Geistesgeschichte*). Perhaps few other male theologians have taken the thought and deeds of women in this *Geistegeschichte* so seriously. As Schönborn rightly points out, he considered their experience and their reflections not only as "spirituality" but as theology.[48]

Thérèse of Lisieux, of course, gets particular attention, but he refers also to Teresa of Avila, Mary Magdalene of Pazzi, Angela Merici, Elisabeth of the Trinity, Mary of the Visitation, Lucy of Fatima, Elisabeth of Thüringen, Catherine of Siena, Margaret of Cortona, Gertude, Jeanne de Chantal, Mary of the Incarnation, Mathilde of Magdeburg, Margaret Mary Alacoque, Sophie Barat, Mathilde of Hackeborn, Francesca Romana, Mary Ward, Margaret Ebner, Gemma Galgani, Catherine Labouré, Edith Stein.[49]

On a more contemporary level, he mentions women he knew such as Adrienne von Speyr, Madeleine Delbrêl, Mother Teresa, Chiara Lubich, Gertrud von Lefort and Frederike Görres. In pointing to their experiences we get an indication of how he sees a prophetic role of women in the Church in that he links it to the prophetic dimension of the Marian principle. The women we are introduced to are vibrant personalities of the Church, who have kept before us some key features of the Marian principle.

---

48. See "Il contributo di Hans Urs von Balthasar all'ecumenismo," in K. Lehmann and W. Kasper, *Hans Urs von Balthasar,* 431-450, espec. 449.
49. See the contribution of Adrienne von Speyr's "prayer portraits," *First Glance at Adrienne von Speyr,* 71ff. Cf. Von Speyr, *Das Allerheiligenbuch* 2/1.

On the Reservation of Ministerial Ordination to Men Only [50]

It is his consideration of the Marian principle in the Church that prompts von Balthasar's views on the issue of reservation of ministerial ordination to men only.[51] For him it is not so much a negative no on our Lord's part than a very definite feminine yes on Mary's part that throws light on the issue. Certainly, as Paul writes, in Christ there is neither male nor female (Gal 3:28). What matters is for everyone in the specificity of their vocation "to be Christ." The paradox is that for everyone, male or female, to "be Christ" is to imitate Mary and, in their transparency, allow Christ be formed in them.

Divine revelation, however, does not result in an asexual neutrality of the human condition. Von Balthasar believes that within the realm of the Church, the person-centered height and depth of the sexual difference emerges fully in the light of the Christ-Church relationship. The unity of the two co-constitutive Marian and Petrine profiles also speak of mutuality as a key to unity in distinction. In his personalist ecclesiology, he sees Mary and Peter as mutually subordinate to one another. We shall further look at this in the subsection on the pope, bishops and the Marian principle.

In terms of priestly ordination, von Balthasar comments that to man is assigned the task of *representation* whereas to woman is assigned *being*. Some men are called to "represent" the Lord, shepherd and bridegroom, present to his Church, but always in a way which never allows them to claim any of the divine dignity for themselves. Echoing Bouyer, von Balthasar sees the man-priest, therefore, as being simultaneously both more and less than himself in that as sexual being he only "represents" what he is not (the Lord) and transmits

---

50. See Pope John Paul II's Apostolic Exhortation, *Ordinatio Sacerdotalis*, AAS 86 (1994), 545-548.
51. For the following see *Maria und das Priesteramt; New Elucidations*, 187ff; "Die Würde der Frau," 346-352; *Short Primer*, 88ff; "How weighty is the argument from 'uninterrupted tradition' to justify the male priesthood?" *Communio* 23 (1996), 185-192.

what he does not really possess (the Lord's real presence and sacraments). Woman, on the other hand, reposes in herself and is entirely her own being, that is, the total reality of a created being before God as partner, receiving, bearing, maturing and nurturing his Word in the Spirit.[52]

Von Balthasar rejects a presumptuous or arrogant mysticism of representation.[53] He is not in favor of seeing priests only as "other Christs" inasmuch as this is the vocation of all Christians. In distinguishing between authority (*Vollmacht*) and power (*Macht*), von Balthasar exhorts against exalting the service of bishop and priest in terms of power. It is a misunderstanding of the priesthood to propose it in terms of a power fundamentally inaccessible to women.[54] Clericalism in the Church has indeed at times presented becoming a priest or bishop as a culmination of Church membership. But it is love, not power, which reigns in the Christian economy. Office-holders always have to look to the Marian existential form of holiness and, on the basis of this existential priesthood common to all, exercise their ministerial authority.[55]

---

52. See "Priesthood's 'uninterrupted tradition,'" 190. See Louis Bouyer, *Woman and Man with God* (London, 1960); *Woman in the Church* (San Francisco: Ignatius Press, 1979).
53. "Über das priesterliche Amt" *Civitas* 23 (1968), 794-797, espec. 794.
54. *New Elucidations*, 196.
55. See "Priesthood's 'uninterrupted tradition,'" 151; *Short Primer*, 94; "Die Gegenwart des einen Jesus Christus in der Einheit der Kirche" in Karl Lehmann (ed.), *In der Nachfolge Jesu Christi: Zum Besuch des Papstes* (Freiburg: Herder, 1980), 37-54, here 54.

The Hour of the Laity

Lay people's new awareness of their vibrant role in the Church has been compared by von Balthasar to the awakening of a sleeping giant.[56] He characterizes our era as the "hour of the laity," and it is linked with a new Marian-ecclesial consciousness in the Church. In this new *kairós* or moment of God, marked by a "solidarity with the world," God is now pouring out his grace in a special way upon the lay state in the Church.[57] Already before the Council van Balthasar saw a properly understood Mariology as preparing the way for a new ecclesiology and a new ecclesial consciousness, above all in the laity.

In a sense, von Balthasar considers the lay state almost as the fundamental state in the Church to which the other two states, priesthood and the life of evangelical counsels, are formed by specific differentiations, concretizations and service.[58] For von Balthasar the "type" or model of lay Christianity is, above all, Mary.[59] What he emphasizes is how much lay people's own missionary role is coming to the fore with a rediscovery of the common priesthood and a prophetic role in various fields such as journalism, urbanization, media, ecological issues and political commitments.[60]

By emphasizing the Marian principle, von Balthasar wants to correct any notion of seeing hierarchy at the center of the Church and laity on the margin. It is no longer a question of the laity being merely dependent on the hierarchy's missionary function in the world (as in the past, and perhaps

---

56. *Razing the Bastions*, 39ff; *La Realtà e la Gloria*, 84.
57. *Explorations I: The Word Made Flesh*, 222.
58. *Christian State of Life*, 201ff.
59. See Antonio Sicari, "Figures of the Church," 206.
60. See von Balthasar's article, "Riflessioni per un lavoro sui movimenti laicali nella Chiesa," in (no editor) *I laici e la missione della Chiesa* (Milan: ISTRZA, 1986), 85-106, espec. 92.

explaining why some lay apostolic missionary actions set up by bishops are dying out), but rather of a better appreciation of the laity's own missionary role. Christian perfection is not the preserve of the religious or priestly state, and lay attachment to a Third Order does not suffice for the contemporary lay person.[61]

Von Balthasar notes that unlike the clergy, who approach the Church reality more from the structural side of things, the theological thinking and feeling of the laity (together with members of religious orders), perhaps reflecting the Marian principle to which they are particularly linked, tends to emphasize the elements of the vital development of the Church through the free, charismatic creations of the Holy Spirit:[62]

> The basis of the Church and her structure cannot grow; but the sphere of life, which is formed predominantly by the laity, can indeed grow. The men of the ministry (who, as members, must grow like all the others) are keepers and gardeners of the growth. The duty of the laity is to be the growth and the blossoming that alone can convince the world of the truth of the teaching of Christ.[63]

Von Balthasar recognizes that there can be tension between laity and ministers, but the criterion of discernment is always whether one's action or criticism is with a view to building up unity in love of the whole Church. In a Marian spirit, criticism comes from love and is ordered toward building up the body in unity.[64] Here, too, von Balthasar proposes the saints as a model in that they provide new forms of life which show the way rather than simply pointing to the faults of others.

---

61. *I laici e la missione della Chiesa*, 91.
62. *Man in History*, 120.
63. *Explorations II: Spouse of the Word*, 315-331, here, 331.
64. *Explorations IV: Spirit and Institution*, 155-156, 207-208; *Office of Peter*, 313ff; *Die Wahrheit ist symphonisch*, 116-120.

Ecclesial Movements, Associations, and Communities

As an astute commentator on the contemporary situation of the Church, von Balthasar was keenly attentive to what was blossoming in the Church's garden. He was particularly attracted by the unprecedented flowering and multiplication in this century of secular institutes, lay associations and ecclesial movements. He himself dedicated much energy to promoting secular institutes and was a friend of the Communion and Liberation Movement.[65] They are a clear expression of what we referred to above (see chapter "Holiness, Saints, Founders and Charisms") as the "new forms" of Church life that emerge through the Spirit's outpouring of charisms in each new age.

He cites Charles de Foucauld's words to indicate the Marian style of these new groups and movements.[66] The Marian disposition of movements and communities such as the Little Brothers and Sisters of Charles de Foucauld or Abbé Pierre's movement appeals to him.[67] It is not a case of these movements or their members wanting to lead the Church, but rather of their "feeling" themselves to be the Church (*sentire ecclesiam*), and so, in a Marian manner, bring the enlightening spirit of the Church into the world. Von Balthasar sees them as

---

65. *Razing the Bastions, passim; Sponsa Verbi*, 25ff; *Der Laie und der Ordensstand* (Einsiedeln, 1948); "Wesen und Tragweite der Säkularinstitute," *Civitas* 11 (1956), 196-210; "Die Theologie des Rätestandes," in S. Richter (ed.), *Wagnis und Nachfolge* (Paderborn: Ferdinand Schöningh, 1964), 9-57; "Das Wagnis der Säkularinstitute," *Internationale Katholische Zeitschrift Communio* 10 (1981), 238-245; *In Gottes Einsatz Leben* (Einsiedeln: Johannes Verlag, 1971) [dedicated to Luigi Giussani and the Communion and Liberation Movement]; "Riflessioni per un lavoro sui movimenti laicali."

66. *Explorations II: Spouse of the Word*, 25. See also Madeleine Delbrêl's work translated and introduced by von Balthasar, *Frei für Gott: über Laien-Gemeinschaften in der Welt* (Einsiedeln: Johannes Verlag, 1976).

67. *Explorations I: The Word Made Flesh*, 222-223.

one of the main causes of hope for the Church's future, because they are a positive source of Church renewal.

These movements also contain new forms of consecrated life in the world. The combination of secularity and consecration appeals to von Balthasar, because the era we live in calls for the Church not to be closed or separated from the world by a wall, and yet, in its openness, it must be rooted in its stand in God.

The "world communities" which are emerging are new expressions in the Church's life. Von Balthasar considers that they are at the very heart and center of the Church precisely because they are arising within the subjective Marian polarity of the Church.[68] Indeed, his own thought on the Marian principle has been deemed a significant contribution to theological reflection on their place in the Church.[69] He affirms that these modern movements are not the products of the Church on the basis of considerations of necessity.[70] They are not constructions of the institution:

> The origins of movements, the large movements, that is, those that have played an important role in the history of the Church, do not lie with the hierarchy. Rather they begin with a lay person consecrated to God, or perhaps a priest, people who, moved by the Spirit, move, act, and found a movement.[71]

While their origins are lay, these new movements are distinguished by their unproblematic attitude to the Church. They recognize the Church as the protectress of what they seek — the authentic revelation of God in Jesus Christ. In saying this, von Balthasar links them with the Marian principle in the Church but also distinguishes them from the more

---

68. See von Balthasar, "Die Nachfolge Christi im Neuen Testament" in Barbara Alrecht and Hans Urs von Balthasar, *Nachfolge Jesu Christi mitten in der Welt* (Meitingen: Kryios Verlag, 1971), 11-26, espec. 17.
69. Libero Gerosa, "Secular institutes, lay associations, and ecclesial movements in the theology of Hans Urs von Balthasar," *Communio* 17 (1990), 343-361, espec. 346.
70. "Riflessioni per un lavoro sui movimenti," 85ff.
71. *La Realtà e la Gloria*, 202.

devotion-oriented Marian movements that developed between the seventeenth to nineteenth centuries. The modern movements are rather a form of Marian engagement in the world. As such they are an expression of the Holy Spirit's pouring out of charisms to respond to the needs of today.[72]

Important in these new movements is their communitarian aspect. The communitarian formation of their members is an "ecclesiasticizing" moment in the sense that it is linked to the formation of a Marian ecclesial soul (*anima ecclesiastica*). The community forms the individual to work as an ecclesial person; it is the place where what von Balthasar calls the "ecclesial aspect" of a Christian's life is examined, verified and continuously rectified.[73] All of this is important because the movements and new communities are like a cohesive point in the Church. They too carry out a Marian role by being an expression of the Church's unity and universality, carrying out a modern mission in the Church.[74]

---

72. *La Realtà e la Gloria,* 83.
73. *Explorations IV: Spirit and Institution,* 288.
74. *Rechenschaft 1965* (Einsiedeln: Johannes Verlag, 1965), 13; *La Realtà e la Gloria,* 177-178.

The Pope, Bishops and the Marian Principle

In his homily at von Balthasar's funeral, Cardinal Joseph Ratzinger praised von Balthasar's combination of great respect for the Petrine, hierarchical structure of the Church with the knowledge that it is not the whole Church nor her deepest element.[75] He understood that the objective holiness of hierarchical ministry is no substitute for a lack of subjective holiness on the part of ministers.[76] The Marian principle points to the primacy of holiness for everyone in the Church, be they office holders or not.

It might be said that the full recognition of the Marian principle brings with it a certain relativization of the hierarchical element in the Church. Von Balthasar did not intend such a relativization as negation or undervaluing of the hierarchical dimension of the Church.[77] What he proposes is a rediscovery of the Petrine institutional element within the all-embracing Marian principle in the Church.

The institutional element of the Church is relative to love. The hierarchy and sacraments are means toward the Marian holiness of love in the Church. This is her "supra-ministerial" heart and the basis of her mission in the world. The hierarchy and sacraments serve this holiness; they are not an end in themselves as the fact that they will cease in paradise reminds us.

Office-bearing ministers must themselves strive toward their particular form of the universal call to holiness. This will involve their listening to and appreciating the voice of the Spirit in the lived holiness of the Church. Just as saints need

---

75. See "Homily at the Funeral Liturgy for Hans Urs von Balthasar" *Communio* 15 (1988), 512-516.
76. Cf. *Verbum Caro*, 198ff; *Sponsa Verbi*, 27.
77. Cf. Brian McNeil, "The Exegete as Iconographer: Balthasar and the Gospels" in John Riches (ed.), *The Analogy of Beauty*, 134-146, espec. 137, fn. 7.

humility to be measured by the formal norms and judgement of the Church, because the Spirit is the Spirit of the Church, so too the occupants of Church office need the humility to be enlightened by the Spirit of Christ shining forth in the norms of holiness lived within the Church.[78]

Commenting specifically on the office of the papacy, von Balthasar's writings promote the Marian principle precisely with a view to "integrating" the papacy in the Church as a whole. He believes that the greater the degree to which the Marian communion in the Church is lived, the greater the support of the Petrine role. The papacy is a charism of unity in the Church. If Christians as a body do not supply the witness to unity that a function like that of the papacy is designed to promote, such a function is in vain.[79] In an interesting observation, he interprets the growing number of Papal encyclicals as an expression of a newly emerging Marian profile of the papacy itself. In recent decades it is as if the pope contributes his word in a maternally helpful manner to the discussion concerning today's world problems.[80]

With regard to Pope John Paul II, von Balthasar points to the primacy of his Christian witness that radiates from the Office over and beyond the promulgation of official texts.[81] He also admires the centrality of theme of the Marian principle in this pope's life and writings. Guido M. Miglietta has further commented that "Hans Urs von Balthasar's theology has certainly contributed to reflection on the theme of the Marian profile of the Church, which emerges in the teaching of John Paul II."[82]

---

78. See *Theologie der Geschichte*, 82-83.
79. *New Elucidations*, 182.
80. *Razing the Bastions*, 98.
81. See *Test Everything*, 65.
82. Guido M. Miglietta, "Il volto mariano femminile della Chiesa secondo Hans Urs von Balthasar" *Theotokos* 5 (1997), 265-282, espec. 278.

Ecumenism and Inter-Religious Dialogue

While not directly involved in "official" ecumenism of commissions and discussions, von Balthasar did play a significant part in the twentieth century ecumenical movement. Peter Henrici tells us that at the beginning of the Second World War, his superiors thought of sending him to Rome where he and three other Jesuits were to have established an institute for ecumenical theology. Instead of Rome he ended up in Basel, and there he became a friend of Karl Barth whose theology he presented in a well-acclaimed work.[83] His friendship and dialogue with Karl Barth opened up for him avenues of insight into the goal and ways of ecumenism.

Several of his works (*The Word Made Flesh; The Theology of History; Love, the Way of Revelation*) are the fruit and continuation of this ecumenical discussion.[84] In the original plan of his trilogy, the last volume of *The Glory of the Lord* was to have been an ecumenical conclusion as befitted the ecumenical goal throughout the trilogy. It has been suggested that *In the Fullness of Faith* takes its place.[85]

While his contribution in general in the field of ecumenism has been recognized, Max Schoch, a Swiss Protestant pastor, has pointed to the positive import of von Balthasar's personalistic and symbolic ecclesiology.[86] By pointing to the personal figures of Mary, Peter, John, etc., von Balthasar provides a less abstract basis for ecumenical discussion and promotes a dialogue that looks not to the lowest common

---

83. *The Theology of Karl Barth* (San Francisco: Ignatius Press, 1992). See also K. Barth/H. U. von Balthasar, *Einheit und Erneuerung der Kirche* (Freiburg: Paulusverlag, 1968).
84. See Peter Henrici, "A Sketch of von Balthasar's life," 18.
85. See also *Mein Werk*, 82, and Henrici "A Sketch of von Balthasar's life," 39.
86. See Max Schoch, "Colloquio ecumenico tra fratelli: La via balthasariana all'esercizio della cattolicità," in K. Lehmann and W. Kasper (eds.), *Hans Urs von Balthasar,* 401-430 and "Zum Gedenken an Hans Urs von Balthasar," *Lutherische Monatshefte* (Hamburg) 27 (1988), 395.

denominators but rather to the full gospel forms of how we
"could be" and "should be."[87] Schoch finds von Balthasar's
perspective of the Mary-Peter polarity in the Church a significant help in ecumenical discussion. An interesting aside here is
Jeffrey Kay's observation to the effect that von Balthasar's sen-
sitivity to symbols will possibly help to draw contemporary
theology away from the temptation to settle down in Enlightenment hermeneutics, just at the time when non-theological
thought is making a second Copernican revolution into a
post-critical hermeneutics.[88]

   Christoph Schönborn too contends that von Balthasar's
Mariology is fundamental for the ecumenical dialogue on the
Church.[89] Not that von Balthasar wants Mary to be made the
center of theology. The significance of this woman of the
gospel is that her life speaks of a qualitative rather than a quantitative catholicity.[90] God's great plan in Jesus Christ is to
re-integrate the world into the catholicity of the divine life.[91]
Mary's yes played a key role in this plan, because she was
transparent to Christ and the whole mystery being communicated through him. It is her transparent yes that, in
von Balthasar's view, continues to provide an ecumenical
meeting-point between Catholics, Christians, Jews and
atheists.[92]

   For Christians, Mary's transparency to Christ indicates a
pathway for ecumenism — to be open and attentive to our
common origins, not only in the historical sense of the begin-
nings of Christianity, but in the sense of being open to the ever
new presence of the Risen Lord, who wills to be present to the
Church until the end of time. Mary's own example provides

87. See Schoch, "Colloquio," 411; *Theo-Drama III,* 452ff.
88. See Jeffrey Kay, "Hans Urs von Balthasar: A Post-Critical Theologian?" *Concilium* 141
    (1981), 84-89.
89. Cf. "Hans Urs von Balthasar's Contribution to Ecumenism" in D. Schindler, *Hans Urs
    von Balthasar: His Life and Work,* 251-263, espec. 260. See further T'Joen, "Marie et
    L'ésprit," 192, 194.
90. See his article, "The Claim to Catholicity," *Explorations IV: Spirit and Institution,* 65-121.
91. See "Die Absolutheit des Christentums und die Katholizität der Kirche," in Walter
    Kasper (ed.), *Absolutheit des Christentums* (Freiburg: Herder, 1977), 131-156.
92. See Alfredo Marranzini, "Hans Urs von Balthasar teologo della gloria di Dio nel mondo"
    in *Hans Urs von Balthasar, Abbattere i bastioni* (Turin: Borla, 1966), 7-28, espec. 11.

ecumenical attitudes such as patient openness to the "whole" unity that is to be granted to us "from above" as a gift.

To strive together in a process of simplicity toward a deeper penetration of and convergence in the ever greater truth of revelation is what Mary teaches. Von Balthasar points to the Lutheran and Anglican movements, *Taizé* and *Grandchamps* as examples of striving for the more rather than the less in a unity based on the gospel.[93] It might also be observed here that, linked with what we saw in the previous chapter, ecclesial movements and communities are another significant expression of how the Marian principle comes into play in ecumenism.

Apart from the attitude of transparency to Christ, the Marian principle points to holiness of the gospel lived together as the way to greater unity between the Churches and dialogue with other religions. Through the reciprocal bearing of one another there is an unknown force that greatly contributes to our ecumenical desire. Through much hidden suffering, lived and offered to God in a discipleship modeled upon Mary, ecumenism progresses in ways that we cannot calculate.

There is one final and very important dimension which von Balthasar highlights. And that is the prophetic aspect of the Marian principle in terms of charisms and mysticism. These can be a source of inspiration and direction for ecumenism. Von Balthasar points, for instance, to Thérèse of Lisieux's "little way." It contains elements that meet the demands of the Reformers and of Protestant spirituality.[94] He also refers us in this context to the writings, charism and personality of Adrienne von Speyr, whom he compared to Hildegaard of Bingen. Because of her biblical and mystical emphasis, she (her charism and writings) acts as a meeting point between brothers and sisters in different denominations of the Christian faith.[95]

---

93. See *Convergences: To the Source of Christian Mystery* (San Francisco: Ignatius Press, 1983); *Who is a Christian?* 36-40.
94. See *Two Sisters in the Spirit*, 283.
95. *La Realtà e la Gloria*, 22-24. In this regard, see also Joan Patricia Back, *Il Contributo del Movimento dei Focolari all Koinonia Ecumenica: Una spiritualità del nostro tempo al servizio dell'unità* (Rome: Città Nuova, 1988).

With regard to dialogue with other religions and people of other convictions, von Balthasar also highlights the Marian profile of witness, love and holiness. He points to the witness and work of people like Mother Teresa and Chiara Lubich.[96] Mother Teresa brought love everywhere and so is a model which presents the best access to the gospel message also for people of non-Christian convictions. Chiara Lubich's dialogue with Buddhists (the dialogue von Balthasar considers most difficult) and people of non-Christian convictions is also held up as a model of dialogue in its witness to God who is love.

---

96. See *La Realtà e la Gloria,* 155 and 189.

The Marian Principle and the Church in the World

In the course of an interview, von Balthasar once commented that nobody converts to Christ just because of magisterium, sacrament, clergy, canon law, apostolic nunciatures or a gigantic ecclesiastical machinery.[97] He made this comment not to take from any of these aspects of Church life but rather to emphasize the centrality of the gospel witness lived in the world. What is demanded of Christian love for the Church today is not a love for an entity with defined confines but rather an unconditioned love for Christ, This love begins in the Church and, in the Church, is identified with love for the Lord in our brothers and sisters in the world. The Church is not an end in herself but presupposes the world of creation for her meaning and purpose. She is open to this world in her being and work and pours forth upon it.[98] The world is not to be considered as a separate entity from the Church. On the contrary, the world is the kingdom of God in the process of becoming, and the Church is the yeast at work within it. Today more than ever therefore, writes von Balthasar, we cannot be just "products" of the Church but always the Church producing in service of our brothers and sisters who stand within the realm of grace and redemption. It is her Marian identity that prompts the Church to offer her contribution to the universal search for human wholeness, because the Church understands herself as "human wholeness, Mary."[99]

---

97. *Test Everything,* 18.
98. See "The Layman and the Church," *Explorations II: Spouse of the Word,* 315-331.
99. *Man in History,* 73ff.

What direction does this Marian contribution take today? Henri de Lubac referred to von Balthasar as "perhaps the most cultivated man" of his time and claimed that his spiritual diagnosis of our civilization is the most penetrating to be found.[100] Von Balthasar sees much that is positive in the new desire for simplicity and authenticity, the struggle for justice, and the global planning and working together, especially among young people. Nevertheless, in commenting upon the atheistic humanism of our contemporary world scene, and in echoing a motif from John of the Cross, he suggests that we are living in an era characterized by a kind of collective dark night.[101]

Among the features of this dark night is a predominance of a "masculine" rationalism of the *homo faber,* which has shaped a culture that sees natural things and conditions above all as material for manufacture. Even the human spirit is in danger of becoming material for mere self-manipulation through the various sciences. There is a loss of the wonder of being and, once devoid of philosophy and of ethics, we risk becoming victims of a pure positivism of "making" and "having." A Promothean attitude toward reality creeps in, one in which we find ourselves making an ideal of total cybernetics and an ideology of global technological progress.

Run aground, as Barth writes, on the sandbanks of a technological rationalism, many serious questions face us about the direction we want to take in the future.[102] Precisely because the Church's foundation is in the mystery of God's plan, the Church's consciousness and mission is closely bound with humankind's consciousness and need to rediscover mystery. But the question that we ourselves face is how can the Church best serve humanity and shed some light on the serious questions facing the world today?

---

100. "A Witness of Christ," 229.
101. See *Glory of the Lord V: The Realm of Metaphysics in the Modern Age* (Edinburgh: T&T Clark, 1986), 648.
102. *Convergences: To the Source of Christian Mystery,* 11ff.

A Proposal: Islands of Humanity?

"Love alone is credible" is a title of one of von Balthasar's writings. And love alone is ultimately the response the Church can offer to contemporary issues. In von Balthasar's view, our social, political and economic orders with their globalization and struggle for social justice need to rediscover and be regulated by the "law" of Christian love. There is no quick solution as to how this is to be done, but von Balthasar launches an interesting proposal in the context of a reply to questions concerning Christian culture.[103]

In pointing to the lack of culture in general wrought by the entire pseudo-human bureaucratic machine, von Balthasar surmises that in the prison we have built for ourselves we are witnessing the technical civilization in its final stage. How is a new civilization to be constructed? Recalling the experience of the early Christians, he proposes that Christians today be leaders in building "islands of humanity."[104]

The "islands" von Balthasar writes about are those points where people can experience and rediscover authentic realization and freedom. What he suggests are concrete forms of gospel life and mutual love through which Christians would contribute to the rebuilding of a cultural humanism. They are luminous points of the re-discovery of ultimate meaning as revealed in God's movement to us and our moving with him.[105] This movement centers in Jesus Christ.

Accordingly, the "islands of humanity" that are needed today are those points where the living presence of Jesus among his disciples bears witness to God, because "if Christ remains sacramentally present among us, it is for the sake of

---

103. See *Test Everything*, 50ff.
104. See *Test Everything*, 50. For an interesting comparison, see A. MacIntyre, *After Virtue: A Study in Moral Theory* (Notre Dame: University of Notre Dame Press, 1981), 245. See further Edward Oakes, "Ethics and the Search for God's Will in the Thought of Hans Urs von Balthasar," *Communio* 17 (1990), 409-431; Marc Ouellet, "Hans Urs von Balthasar: Witness to the Integration of Faith and Culture" *Communio* 18 (1991), 111-126.
105. "Response to my critics" *Communio* 5 (1978), 69-76.

the faithful, that they may realize his presence even outside
the sacraments: For where two or three are gathered in his
name, he is in their midst (Mt 18:20)":[106]

> It is not enough to preach the message of salvation to
> the world from outside: this message must permeate it
> like leaven, becoming disseminated throughout it.
> What we are speaking of is — the modern expression
> — "inculturation. . . ." There must be a loving appreci-
> ation of the existing values; it must calmly be shown
> that they are genuinely fulfilled only in the message of
> Christ. . . . The Church can only effectively pursue her
> task, therefore, if she herself alternates between two
> impossible poles: preaching to the world purely from
> without and transforming it from within. As Church,
> she must penetrate without becoming "establish-
> ment" and advance without leaving unfinished busi-
> ness behind.[107]

The "islands of humanity" that von Balthasar proposes can
be viewed as expressions of the living prophetic Marian
dimension in the Church. Since von Balthasar sees Mary as
humanity and creation realized, and since there is a continuing Marian polarity in the Church, we can say that he looks
toward the all-embracing principle of the Church, with its prophetic, charismatic and mystical dimensions, for inspiration
and projects to be pursued by the Church in the world.

The Marian principle points to the primacy of love: love
received, responded to, and shared. The proposal of the
"islands of humanity" could be incarnated in many ways.
Together with Adrienne von Speyr, von Balthasar himself set
up a community of laity and priests, who took John the Evangelist as the primary reference and attempted as a community
to embody in a contemporary life style the relationship
between Mary and John discussed above.

---

106. *Christian State of Life*, 338.
107. *Theo-Drama IV*, 465.

The dialogical style of theology carried out by von Balthasar might also be considered an expression of creating "islands of humanity." He sought out dialogue-partners (such as Claudel, Bernanos, Péguy and others, who themselves participated in the profound social crises of their times) and with them opened up new avenues for radiating the meaning which is seen in the light of Jesus Christ.

Von Balthasar has no sharply defined model for these "islands of humanity." A "collective imagination" is needed to discover new projects and translate them together into action. Clearly, projects associated with the secular institutes, associations, and ecclesial movements can be viewed in this perspective.[108]

Each moment of love for one's neighbor constructs one of those "small islands" and builds up a new civilization of love. But, just as it was for the first Christians, so today too the novelty of Jesus Christ must be proclaimed, not just through individual good example, but through the witness of a new humanity shaped by the new commandment and made manifest on social, economic and political levels.[109]

Mindful of the Second Vatican Council's positive openness expressed in the pastoral constitution on the Church, *Gaudium et Spes,* von Balthasar knows that the law of the death and resurrection is at the heart of any project that strives toward dialogue with the world. The "islands of humanity" are not u-topic nor are they the fruits of our labors alone. Rather, as contemporary expressions of the Marian principle, they have their source in God's initiative and radiate in our being. In the words of Cardinal Ratzinger:

> The Church is not an apparatus; it is not merely institution; she is also not one of the usual sociological figures — she is person. She is a woman. She is mother.

---

108. See Walbert Bühlmann, *Welt Kirche: Neue Dimensionen Model für das Jahr 2001* (Graz: Verlag Styria, 1985) and Bruno Secondin's work, *I Nuovi Protagonisti: Movimenti, associazioni, gruppi nella Chiesa* (Milan: Edizioni Paoline, 1991), espec. 137.
109. *Theo-Drama IV,* 476ff; *Theo-Logik III,* 375ff. See Enrique Cambón, *Trinità, modello sociale* (Rome: Città Nuova, 1999).

She is living. The Marian understanding of the Church
is the most decisive contrast to a merely organizational
or bureaucratic concept of Church. We cannot make
the Church, we must *be* Church. And it is only to the
degree in which faith stamps our being more than our
doing, that *we are* Church, that Church is in us. It is
only in Marian being that we become Church. In her
origins, the Church was not made, but born. She was
born when the *fiat* was aroused in Mary's soul. That is
the deepest desire of the Council: that the Church
awaken in our souls. Mary shows us the way.[110]

Conclusion

At the beginning of a new millennium, there is a rediscovery
or new discovery of this Marian principle. This book has
aimed at opening up something of von Balthasar's intuition
concerning this "sign of our times." Perhaps the next stage of
our reception of the Second Vatican Council will be a further
realization of its significance. "At the dawn of the new millennium," commented John Paul II recently, "we notice with joy
the emergence of the Marian profile of the Church that summarizes the deepest contents of the conciliar renewal."[111]

---

110. "Die Ekklesiologie des Zweiten Vatikanums," *Internationale Katholische Zeitschrift Communio* 15 (1986), 41-52, espec. 52.
111. See his catechesis on signs of hope in the Church, 23 November, 1998.

Bibliography

For a full catalogue of von Balthasar's works, see Cornelia Capol, *Hans Urs von Balthasar: Bibliographies 1925-1990* (Einsiedeln: Johannes Verlag, 1990). The following is a selection of his books and articles in which the theme of the Marian principle in the Church is treated. (Publication info for books and articles from which I have quoted but which are not listed here is provided in the footnote corresponding to the first citation.)

Books

Christian Meditation. San Francisco: Ignatius Press, 1989.

The Christian State of Life. San Francisco: Ignatius Press, 1983.

Elucidations. San Francisco: Ignatius Press, 1998.

Explorations in Theology I: The Word Made Flesh. San Francisco: Ignatius Press, 1989.

Explorations in Theology II: Spouse of the Word. San Francisco: Ignatius Press, 1991.

Explorations in Theology III: Creator Spirit. San Francisco: Ignatius Press, 1993.

Explorations in Theology IV: Spirit and Institution. San Francisco: Ignatius Press, 1995.

First Glance at Adrienne von Speyr. San Francisco: Ignatius Press, 1981.

The Glory of the Lord: A Theological Aesthetics. Vol I: Seeing the Form. San Francisco: Ignatius Press, 1982.

Die Grossen Ordensregeln. Einsiedeln: Benziger Verlag, 1961.

Heart of the World. San Francisco: Ignatius Press, 1979.

Homo Creatus Est: Skizzen zur Theologie V. Einsiedeln: Johannes Verlag, 1986.

In the Fullness of Faith: On the Centrality of the Distinctively Catholic. San Francisco: Ignatius Press, 1988.

Love Alone: the Way of Revelation. San Francisco: Ignatius Press, 1968.

Man in History A Theological Study. London: Sheed and Ward, 1986.

Maria und das Priesteramt. Printed as manuscript: Arnold-Böcklin-Strasse 43, CH-4051 Basel, no date given.

Mary for Today. Middlegreen, Slough: St. Paul Publications, 1987.

Mary, God's Yes to Man: Pope John Paul II's Encyclical Letter, Mother of the Redeemer. San Francisco: Ignatius Press, 1988.

Mysterium Paschale. Edinburgh: T&T Clark, 1990.

New Elucidations. San Francisco: Ignatius Press, 1986.

The Office of Peter and the Structure of the Church. San Francisco: Ignatius Press, 1986.

Our Task. San Francisco: Ignatius Press, 1994.

Prayer. San Francisco: Ignatius Press, 1986.

Razing the Bastions. San Francisco: Ignatius Press, 1993.

La Realtà e la Gloria: Articoli e interviste 1978 – 1988. Milan: EDIT, 1988.

Test Everythhing: Hold Fast to What is Good. San Francisco: Ignatius Press, 1989.

The Threefold Garland: The World's Salvation in Mary's Prayer. San Francisco: Ignatius Press, 1982.

Theo-Drama: Theological Dramatic Theory. Vol. III: Dramatis Personae: Persons in Christ. San Francisco: Ignatius Press, 1992.

Theo-Drama: Theological Dramatic Theory. Vol. IV: The Action. San Francisco: Ignatius Press, 1994.

Theo-Drama: Theological Dramatic Theory. Vol. V: The Last Act. San Francisco: Ignatius Press, 1998.

Theologik III: Der Geist der Wahrheit. Einsiedeln: Johannes Verlag, 1987.

Two Sisters in the Spirit: Thérèse of Lisieux and Elisabeth of the Trinity. San Francisco: Ignatius Press, 1992.

Who is a Christian? New York: Newman Press, 1968.

You Have Words of Eternal Life: Scripture Meditations. San Francisco: Ignatius Press, 1989.

Articles

"Conceived by the Holy Spirit, Born of the Virgin Mary" in Medard Kehl and Werner Löser, *The Von Balthasar Reader*. Edinburgh: T&T Clark, 1982, 140-143.

"Das Katholische an der Kirche" *Kölner Beiträge* 10 (1972), 1-19.

"Epilogue" in Louis Bouyer, *Women in the Church*. San Francisco: Ignatius Press, 1979, 113-121.

"Die Erscheinung der Mutter" *Schweizer Rundschau* 44 (1944/5), 73-82.

"Heilig öffentlich Geheimnis" *Internationale Katholische Zeitschrift Communio* 7 (1978), 1-12.

"In Retrospect" in John Riches (ed.), *The Analogy of Beauty: The Theology of Hans Urs von Balthasar*. Edinburgh: T&T Clark, 1986, 194-221.

"Die marianische Prägung der Kirche" in Wolfgang Beinert (ed.), *Maria heute ehren*. Freiburg: Herder, 1977, 263-279.

"Maria in der kirchlichen Lehre und Frömmigkeit" in Joseph Ratzinger and Hans Urs von Balthasar, *Maria-Kirche in Ursprung*. Freibug im Breisgau: Herder, 1980, 41-79.

"Maria und der Geist" *Geist und Leben* 56 (1983), 173-177.

"Our Lady in Monasticism" *Word and Spirit* 10 (1988), 52-56.

"Verstehen oder Gehorchen?" *Stimmen der Zeit* (Freiburg) 69 (1938), 73-85.

"Die Würde der Frau" *Internationale Katholische Zeitschrift Communio* 11 (1982), 346-352.

Index of Names